Buddha never raised kids & Jesus didn't drive carpool

Praise for

Buddha Never Raised Kids
and Jesus Didn't Drive Carpool

Parenting can be our most rewarding
and sometimes our most difficult task in our lifetime.
Vickie has done a brilliant job of helping us be more calm
in the vast array of storms parenting brings to us.

— **KATHRYN KVOLS,**
author of *Redirecting Children's Behavior*

In *Buddha Never Raised Kids*,
Vickie Falcone brings the wisdom of the ages to the parents of today.
This book belongs on every family's bookshelf.

— **GAY HENDRICKS, PH.D.,**
co-author (with Kathlyn Hendricks) of
Conscious Loving and *The Conscious Heart*

The ideas Vickie shares work not only
for parent/child relationships, but also for all relationships.
Vickie writes from experience with wit, humor, and vivid practicality
to help parents realize it's never too late to parent with soul.
A must read for dynamic parenting in the new millennia.

— **REV. MERLE MEANS,**
Church of Religious Science and motivational speaker

Vickie Falcone is focused on applied enlightenment,
the practical aspects for living in a present and contactful way
in the real world, where there are children and other people
you have responsibility for and responsiveness to. She is saying,
"Buddha never raised kids and Jesus didn't drive carpool, but by God
I have, and I imagine if they had, this is how they would have done it!
They would both have been centered in themselves, related to gravity
and grounded in being first and intentionally directly connected
and in contact with their kids right after that, and everything else
that happened in family life would come from
that groundedness and relatedness."
The title is not the only thing that is funny about this book!
It's a wonderful book!

— **BRAD BLANTON, PH.D.,**
author of *Radical Parenting: Seven Steps to a Functional Family in a Dysfunctional World*

VICKIE FALCONE

JODERE
GROUP

Buddha never raised kids & Jesus didn't drive carpool

Seven Principles for Parenting with Soul

JODERE
G R O U P

Published by Jodere Group, Inc.
P.O. Box 910147, San Diego, CA 92191-0147
800.569.1002 | www.jodere.com

Book design by Charles McStravick
Editorial supervision by Chad Edwards

Library of Congress Cataloging-in-Publication Data

Falcone, Vickie.
Buddha never raised kids and Jesus didn't drive carpool :
seven principles for parenting with soul / Vickie Falcone
p. cm.
ISBN 1-58872-062-4
1. Parenting—Religious aspects. I. Title.

BL625.8 .F35 2003
291.4'41--dc21

2002034109

ISBN 1-58872-062-4
06 05 04 03   4 3 2 1
First printing, June 2003

dedication

To my daughters, Brianna and Alexa.
I humbly acknowledge you
as my spiritual teachers.
Thank you for your patience and love
as I continue to learn.

To Joe, my husband and friend.
You saw the light in me when I could not
and helped me heal.
I am forever grateful.

To my mother, Pat.
You loved me unconditionally
And created the space for my transformation.

contents

acknowledgments

Throughout the process of bringing this book to life, I felt overwhelmed by the love, support, and generosity of many friends, colleagues, and family members who believed in this book and helped it become a reality.

Kathryn Kvols taught me most of what I know about parenting and started me on this special path. Through teaching the work found in her book, *Redirecting Children's Behavior,* I grew to be a better parent and person. She continually inspires me to higher parenting planes.

From the very start, my friend Carolyn Golbus offered endless streams of encouragement and vast amounts of time. Her superb organization skills helped me through many a dark night when it all seemed too much to manage.

I feel blessed to work with Winnie Shows. She is an immensely talented writer who transformed my words into an inspiring message. Her devotion, integrity, and ability to keep me focused constantly inspired me. Winnie's passionate insistence that parents needed to read what I needed to write moved me deeply.

The love and guidance I received from the Parenting with Soul focus group gave me the courage to bring this message to a larger audience.

Thank you to: Bertha Campbell, Debbie Cerri, Lisa Chiles, Aluna Flis, Nancy Kimbrell, Kristen Lassalette, Leslie Lebendiger, Beth Mobilian, Leah Moriarty, Eileen Seeley, and Julie Wagner. I feel grateful for your honest feedback, your wise counsel, and for helping me find my voice.

Paul Schadler, M.D., produced my first audio tape series and encouraged me to write the book. His belief in this message touched me deeply.

Bill Reidler of Global Relationship Centers lovingly coaxed me far beyond my comfort level and into a life of passion and peace. Marc LeBlanc is another comfort zone buster to whom I am forever grateful, and Judy Sabah's superb coaching skills helped me balance my life with grace.

To the many participants in my parenting seminars over the last decade who provided the ultimate forum in which I learned to be a better parent. You so openly shared your most intimate challenges and successes and moved me to continually grow as a parent and a speaker.

To the members of the Colorado Chapter of the National Speakers Association and to all of the speakers who shared your journey through your presentations there, thank you. Your messages reached me and ushered me into a grander vision of myself as a speaker.

Bonnie Solow was everything I could have wished for in an agent: enthusiastic, professional, and highly skilled at her art. Thank you to my publisher Debbie Luican and the caring staff at Jodere Group who heartily embraced this project.

My mother, Pat, dropped everything to spend a week with my children when I was on an important deadline, and she has always encouraged me to follow my dream. I am surely blessed to have her as my teacher and mother. My brother Douglas led our family down our first path of healing, which changed my life. For that I am forever grateful. For as long as I can remember, my father, Jim, saw me as supremely competent. Thank you, Dad, for motivating me to reach for your big vision of who I could be.

One of my biggest challenges was writing this book without neglecting my family. Many people rallied to help. In the very beginning, Katie Wright lovingly cared for my children and created much-needed space and peace of mind. Later, many friends mobilized to remind me to care for myself and provide my children with loving care. Thank you to everyone who graciously offered an abundance of sleepovers and play dates.

From designing the original book cover (at age eight) to offering insightful editing advice (at age eleven), my daughter Brianna was a powerful positive force behind this book. My daughter Alexa offered her unique form of support by bringing many a smile to my weary face. Her sense of humor and special spirit continually lifted *my* spirit and lightened the load at just the right moment. Both Alexa and Brianna cheered wildly for my successes, increasing my joy tenfold. My children provided the motivation for writing this book and for my intensely satisfying journey of spiritual growth. I feel grateful without end that they choose me to be their mom; their essence graces every page.

Through the years-long process of writing the book, my husband, Joe, never uttered a discouraging word. Not one. He believed in me and enthusiastically supported my vision. His steadfast love and respect sustained me on this journey. His lighthearted approach to life inspired me to relax into well-being.

My deepest gratitude to my Creator, whose divine inspiration is the reason this book exists. I prayed for road signs and You delivered. I prayed for help and You sent it. I offered prayers of gratitude and You showered me with blessings far beyond anything I was able to anticipate. May this and all of my endeavors honor You.

I was a really great parent before I had kids. I believe the last time I had all the answers I was pregnant with my first child. In the grocery store I would observe a harried mother saying, "Here, Trevor, I'll buy you the candy if you'll promise to stop running in the aisles." *Ha! I'll never cave in like that mother,* I'd think as I flashed Trevor's mom a smile laced with self-righteous pity. In the next aisle I'd hear, "Brittany, you get over here this instant! Do you want a spanking, young lady?" I'd say to myself, *No way will I ever be that harsh with my precious child!* as I smugly stroked my swelling belly.

The one thing I promised myself I would *never* do was yell at my child. No way. I wasn't going to yell at my children the way my parents yelled at me. *Never.*

How old do you think she was when I first broke *that* promise?

Ten months.

She was sitting on the living room floor, not even walking yet, and I was screaming in her face. I will never forget the fear in her eyes or how she was still trying to catch a breath between her sobs an hour later, sitting in her high chair at lunch.

1

I had broken my promise to myself in a big way. *How could you yell at a baby?* I wondered, nearly distraught. I might have been able to rationalize losing it if she were two. Yes, the terrible twos. That would almost be understandable, but not a crawling baby. I suddenly wished I had Trevor and Brittany's moms' phone numbers. Perhaps they'd have something to teach me. Or at least I could apologize for my smugness a year earlier.

Without a major intervention like therapy, a personal growth course, or a recovery program, most of us will parent the way we were parented. We do what feels *familiar*. Like *family*. It's no accident that these words have the same Latin root—a word that meant *the members of a household, including the servants*. Many of us are slaves to our past.

I felt particularly troubled that day because I had embarked on a path of personal and spiritual growth, and parenting seemed to bring out the exact opposite in me. I would read self-help books by night, commit to being a more peaceful person, then fall back into the same disturbing patterns each day.

Things changed quickly after my yelling episode. I realized I could not will myself to parent differently from the way I'd been parented. I needed help, and for someone used to being successful in my career and the "hero" of the family, that realization came hard.

THE JOURNEY BEGINS

I called a psychotherapist friend and he recommended a book called *Redirecting Children's Behavior* by Kathryn Kvols. I devoured it and began to make meaningful changes. A year later I trained to become a parenting instructor and started offering five-week parenting courses in the Aspen area based on Kathryn Kvols' work.

The principles I learned and taught rocked my world. I nearly fried all my synapses as I systematically deconstructed everything I thought I knew about parenting. At times it was not pretty. As I fully realized the shortcomings of the parenting practices I had inherited and was about to pass along to my own children, I felt as if I should turn in my parenting permit, but there seems to be a no-return policy on kids. I had thought I could take the express elevator to enlightenment. Instead, I found it in everyday practices like telling bedtime stories, soothing crying babies, and practicing mindfulness while listening to six-year-olds tell the same knock-knock joke over and over.

I gradually began to incorporate the messages I was teaching into my daily life and over time I became a better parent. Every week before I taught the evening course, I immersed myself in the material, eventually trying out all the ideas on my family before asking the parents in my class to do the same. I worked on the material and it worked on me. I fell on my face a lot, but I was determined to "walk my talk" as much as I could. On more than one occasion, I'd vault into the kitchen and tell my husband, Joe, "I'm teaching conflict resolution tonight, so we need to try it out right now!"

The changes happened slowly. I usually taught classes on Thursday nights and I noticed that I was a really great parent on Fridays! At some point the positive parenting practices spilled over to Saturday. Eventually, I was even a good parent on the preceding Wednesday in anticipation of the class! I often wondered if my husband or children noticed this pattern. I imagined them all huddling together saying, "It's Thursday, let's ask her to make chicken tacos tonight . . . or for more allowance today!"

As the years went by, I learned and grew right along with my students, and each course brought a deeper appreciation of the key practices. We found out how to offer our children choices, acknowledge their feelings, and minimize internecine power struggles. We developed skills to deal with sibling rivalry, family meetings, and conflict resolution. In the process, I began to experience in my life philosopher Joseph Joubert's maxim, *to teach is to learn twice*. I just hadn't realized it sometimes meant doing massive amounts of homework as well.

After several years teaching these parenting programs, I began a search to learn even more about how human consciousness works. I wanted to understand the *why* behind all the *how to's*

I'd been teaching. I wanted to know not only steps 1, 2, and 3 of effective parenting, but the *attitude required* to become a truly great parent. I hungered not only for the words, but the *state of mind* required to develop meaningful relationships with my children.

I got my answers as I read the works of some of the masters of consciousness, including Napoleon Hill, Earl Nightingale, and His Holiness the Dalai Lama. I studied *A Course in Miracles*. I dove into various ancient teachings, including Christianity, Buddhism, Sufism, Islam, and Jewish mysticism for more clues to effective parenting. Contemporary masters like Byron Katie, Gay Hendricks, and Wayne Dyer added practical elements to the mix as did the great pioneers of positive parenting: Rudolf Dreikurs, Haim Ginott, and others. Friends and relatives involved in various 12-step programs like Alcoholics Anonymous shared slogans and ideas that echoed the spiritual principles I was discovering.

I felt motivated and inspired as I began to realize that, in many ways, *all the great teachers, in their different languages and traditions, were speaking about the same core metaphysical concepts.* In the words of Cesar Chavez, "It was all done by Christ and Gandhi and Dr. King. They did it all. We don't have to think about new ideas; we just have to implement what they said, just get the work done."

In the beginning, I struggled as I attempted to apply my new-found knowledge to the real world problems of parenting. How exactly *do* you, as *A Course in Miracles* states, "see the peace instead of this," when the kids are ripping each other's hair out in the back of the car? How do you practice Zen Buddhism's "mindfulness" when it's midnight and you still face three loads of unfolded laundry and a sink full of dirty dishes? And how do you follow Gandhi's exhortation to "be the change you wish to see in the world" when you're running on two hours of sleep and your hubby would like some, uh, attention?

I was clumsy at first, but eventually life got easier as I learned to apply age-old wisdom—along with a dash of humor and lightheart-edness—to everyday parenting challenges. Out of my struggles and successes emerged my own parenting class called Parenting with Soul. This course combined the practical wisdom I'd gathered over the previous ten years with spiritual principles that helped parents who:

- **Feel discouraged**

- **Have disconnected from Source or inner being**

- **Feel frustrated about how hard it is to parent these days**

- **Automatically parent from old patterns**

- **Understand spiritual principles but don't know how to apply them to parenting**

- **Feel they are on a generally good path, yet want to parent with a higher consciousness**

A BOOK IS BORN

About four years after I started teaching parenting courses, I began to receive invitations to speak to conferences and groups around the country. One day while preparing a Parenting with Soul keynote speech, I was reviewing quotes from the Dalai Lama, Buddha, and Jesus, when I suddenly said out loud, "Hey, none of these guys raised kids! No wonder it's so easy for them to spew messages about peace and centeredness. They've never had to drive a carpool of screaming children through a traffic jam or get their two-year-old to eat her veggies!"

Buddha Never Raised Kids and Jesus Didn't Drive Carpool— was it too irreverent a title for my talk? As I tested it on friends and students of different faiths, it seemed to strike a happy chord, and no lightning struck me, so I figured it was okay. I felt deep respect for the work of these and other masters, and now I felt even more committed to synthesize the wisdom from their teachings and apply it to my everyday parenting challenges.

THE SEVEN PRINCIPLES

While distilling these lofty spiritual teachings down to their simplest terms, seven principles emerged, along with practical applications parents can use to deal with everything from bedtime battles to fussy eaters.

- **Connect: With your source, yourself, and your child. This is the heart of parenting with soul.**

- **Awaken Your Intuition: Learn to hear your soul's messages so you're guided to the right action.**

- **Become a Conscious Creator: Master the Law of Attraction to manifest the parenting results you want.**

- **Live in Integrity: Parent on higher ground when you live in impeccable honesty and keep your commitments.**

- **Transform Your Life with Gratitude: Make gratitude second nature and transform your life.**

- **Create Abundance: Model for our children that life is rich and there is enough.**

- **Infuse Your Life with Peace: Joyfully accept life on life's terms to create more peace at home and in the world.**

THE FAR-REACHING EFFECTS OF PARENTING WITH SOUL

I've wondered for years why there's no *Complete Idiot's Guide to Parenting*. Perhaps because most of us might feel embarrassed to purchase a book with that title. And yet most parents I've met (including myself) often feel bewildered and overwhelmed by the challenge of parenting. In many ways, this book will take the pressure off by showing you how to grow and change while being gentle with yourself. In these pages you will be reminded of the importance of nurturing yourself and given permission to do so.

In addition, instead of bombarding you with yet another set of "expert advice" that you must strictly follow, you will learn how to grow your confidence by awakening and listening to your inner guidance.

Like many other parenting books, you will find "to do's." But they are designed to challenge you to move into a higher level of "being." The rewards will be both immediate and long-term. The book is not a quick fix *and* it contains some quick fixes that will have a dramatic and immediate impact on your family. This is a *practice*. Not everything has a 1-2-3 solution, even though much of the information is presented in 1-2-3 format. Ultimately, you'll measure your success by only one gauge: the increasing level of joy in your home.

My quest for world peace led me right back to my living room and ultimately to my soul—my deepest and most authentic self—and the place where I have the greatest impact. I've stumbled and fallen many times, as I wholeheartedly lived the Japanese proverb, "Fall seven times, stand up eight." But over time I've incorporated the messages of the masters into the very fiber of my family. You can, too. If you will supply the desire to grow, I'll provide the exceedingly practical steps and we can begin together today to create more harmony in our homes. You will be rewarded for your effort by seeing your highest vision of yourself as a parent begins to unfold. As Dr. Haim Ginott has said, "It's hard to learn a new language. For one thing, you will always speak with an accent, but for your children, it will be their native tongue."

I give thanks to all the spiritual masters who brought these principles into the world and inspired this book and invite them to walk with us on this journey.

Principle #1

Connect

1

happy parent, happy child

The most important gift
we can give another person
is our own inner peace.

— GERALD JAMPOLSKY, M.D.,
TEACH ONLY LOVE

Connection is the heart of parenting with soul, and the first connection you must make is with your Source and yourself. The last time you flew, you no doubt heard the flight attendant's instructions: "In the event of an emergency, first put on your oxygen mask, then help your child." The airline people know the great secret to successful parent-child relationships: *Parents must first take care of themselves.* Mom and Dad can best support and care for their child only if they are conscious.

We can only give our children what we possess, so it's essential that we make it a priority to nourish and connect with ourselves on all levels. As parents, we can get so busy caring and providing for our families that we forget to care and provide for ourselves. Did you do something today that helped you feel nurtured, loved, connected, and fulfilled? If so, congratulations! You probably already have a good idea of what helps you connect to yourself. If not, it's possible you just haven't seen the importance of taking the time for connection in the context of your family's well being.

When we nurture ourselves, we naturally feel more peaceful, joyful, and wise. And isn't that what we want? We don't have to memorize every parenting book or become a Ph.D. to be a good parent; we just have to connect with our self. When we feel connected, we radiate joy, and people love to be around us. When we feel connected, we have more to give and we also serve as powerful positive role models for our children. When we connect, we become more resourceful, seeing new options and creative solutions.

The most important thing you can do for yourself and your family is to nurture yourself, and from that place of connection, connect with your family. There's no more important piece of advice I can give you to dramatically improve the climate of your home.

I know it's easy to overlook this truth. When the house is a mess and your big goal for the day is to find time to take a shower, it's tempting to go unconscious. You must take the time, however, to get centered and connected for three important reasons. First, there will be more of you to bring to your child: more joy, love, patience, and connection. Second, children learn primarily through modeling. If you take care of yourself, you're more likely to raise a child who knows how to take care of herself, and how to connect to her inner self and to others. Third, we train people how to treat us. I first heard this truth from Wayne Dyer and have watched it play out time after time in my life. If you respect yourself, your child is more likely to respect you as well.

THE SECRET OF THE PEACEFUL MOMMY: FIVE PRACTICES TO CONNECT WITH YOURSELF

Embrace these five practices and connecting with yourself will become a way of life:

1. Give Yourself Permission

Go to your calendar for this week. Do you see any "take care of yourself" appointments? I'll bet you've scheduled several "take care of the children" items. If you do not find at least one self-care item, please give yourself permission to start taking care of number one.

For many parents, especially moms, the simple practice of connecting with ourselves is all but absent in our busy lives, partly because our society places little value on it, and partly because we don't realize how powerful and crucial it is. You may be thinking, *Vickie, this sounds great and I believe you, but I'm running from the time I wake up until I fall into bed at night. Send me a nanny for a year and then I'll connect! I'll also catch up on my romance novels, eat bon bons, and still have time to be a perfect parent.*

I understand why you might resist the idea of adding one more thing to your already overflowing plate. I also intimately understand the demands and time challenges of being a parent. Most importantly, I know and have reaped the benefits of what Cheryl Richardson, author of *Take Time for Your Life,* calls "extreme self care."

In 1994, I was a stay-at-home mom with a six-month-old and a three-year-old. My husband worked 12 and 16 hour days, and in the winter season he would work six or seven days a week. On top of this crazy schedule, I was overweight, ill, and sleep-deprived from nursing an underweight baby every two hours. On top of that, money was also extremely tight. Self-care seemed like an outrageous luxury.

Luckily for me, my extended family intervened. They sat me down and demanded that I commit to doing something to regain my sanity. After much discussion, we decided to purchase a used baby jogger and I committed to taking the girls for daily walks along a lovely stretch of road near my home. The $300 price tag was a lot for us at the time, but I have perhaps never received more value from another object in my life.

On the days I took my walk, I felt transformed. I was happier, felt refreshed, and as a bonus, became slimmer. In just under an hour a day I was now caring for my body, mind, and spirit. At the same time, my children's bodies were receiving fresh air, their minds were getting a break from the house, and their spirits were full of joy and connection to nature. I still walk that road today and often say, "I left twenty pounds (and a lot of aggravation) on that road."

We live in a society that focuses on tangible results. Taking care of yourself is an intangible practice that can, in the beginning, go against everything you've been taught about which activities are valuable and worthy. That's why you must take the initiative and give yourself permission to nurture yourself. When we do, the short- and long-term results will speak for themselves in terms of the sustainable joy in your home. Hang in there.

When we don't plan for the activities that nurture us, we steal time for them. When we don't connect with ourselves, we begin manipulating events to rob moments when we could connect with our children. One summer I took my daughters to the pool two different times so I'd have time to paint my nails. I never even got into the water, and they didn't seem to mind too much. However, the next time I announced we were going to the pool, one of my children said, "I'm not going. You don't play with us. You never even get wet!" I realized that, because I'd been neglecting myself, I ended up neglecting them.

Another time, I put the girls into the bathtub so I could have a long conversation with my friend on the phone. Bath time is usually a fun, connected time for us. If I had made time earlier in the week to connect with my friend, I wouldn't have had to steal it from my kids. I've also taken the kids to the park or put on a video so I could read or do something else I craved. These are not harmful occasional practices. Sometimes I don't feel like going into the pool or watching a video my girls are eager to see. The real question is: Has this become a lifestyle, your practice, your way of life?

What stops you from practicing "extreme self-care?" Guilt? Overwhelm? Time constraints? A belief that parents must make sacrifices? Undervaluing yourself? It's important that you answer this question and move past whatever is holding you back.

One of my favorite parts of teaching my parenting class is that I get to be the "permission giver." When I stand up in front of the class on the first night, I explain the benefits of connecting with yourself and give homework for the upcoming week. It's inspiring to see parents at the second class; many of the participants have practiced taking care of Mom or Dad first. It's even more powerful when couples attend, because they both hear the "take care of yourself" mandate and can support one another in making this a priority.

2. Find Center

Finding center means discovering that "still, quiet space" inside yourself where you feel present, peaceful, and grounded. From center you are able to make the best decisions and make room for inspiration and guidance. How do you find center? Obviously, it's different for everyone. What's important is that you identify whatever it is that helps you feel connected and commit to this practice—especially when life gets hectic. The benefits are huge and show up in practical ways.

I do a few things everyday that help me establish center. Just after I wake up, I take some quiet time to meditate and to set my intention for the day. Another powerful practice for me is to get some exercise. It takes different forms on different days: hiking, biking, weight lifting, yoga, or walking. When I skip this practice, I can feel the difference all day long. I call this short "must-do" list the *Happy Mommy List* (as does my family!). Judy Sabah, speaker, author, and professional coach, refers to this list as the "Ten Daily Habits" each of us should identify to uplift and energize us. Here is what my list looks like:

THE HAPPY MOMMY LIST

Sit in silence
Exercise
Drink 70 oz. of water
Connect with Joe (my husband)
Connect with the children
Write
Be in nature
Eat five fruits and veggies
Avoid refined sugar
Avoid wheat (I'm allergic)

It's really simple. When I do these things, life works. My spirit soars. I'm happier, and that happiness colors all of my experiences, parenting and otherwise. When I don't practice these things, every part of life seems more difficult.

I posted this list on my bathroom mirror as a reminder. The first time my kids saw it, they laughed and teased me. "You have to put up a Happy Mommy List? What's your problem? You can't remember these things?" Even as they laugh and tease, they are learning powerful, positive lessons about the importance of taking care of themselves first. Your list may look different. Here's the practice my friend Carolyn follows:

- **Exercise**

- **Talk with my husband about stuff (parenting, scheduling, trips)**

- **Appreciate**

- **Envision the future (get clear about what I want)**

- **Organize/clean my house**

- **Talk to friends**

- **Relax**

- **Journal/write**

- **Read**

- **Sing/dance**

My husband, Joe, was also willing to share some of the items on his list:

- **Connect with Vickie**

- **Ski in the winter or be outside in summer**

- **Talk to a lot of friends and business associates in person**

- **Kiss my family every time we come and go**

- **Eat at least one meal with my family**
- **Make people smile**
- **Watch SportsCenter**
- **Solve at least one problem**

One of my friends says her daily bath makes the difference in her connectedness with herself. Another says it's riding her horse. For my husband, it's skiing. For another dad, it's brewing the perfect cup of chai tea in solitude and watching the sun come up, enjoying the quiet of the house as his family sleeps.

What good thing do you do for yourself each day? How do you best care for the caretaker? What are your essential practices for staying centered? Ten practices may feel overwhelming. If this is new to you, start with one or two. Discover what centers you and commit to doing it everyday.

3. Start Small

One January morning at my aerobics class, the instructor asked everyone to share their New Year's resolution. Each person took a turn sharing his or her hopes and dreams for the coming year, and when it was my turn I announced, "I will finish my book, start a healing center, and save the world." *Yes, nice lofty spiritual goals for the coming year.* I felt proud. Then it came time for the instructor to share. This mother of two enthusiastically announced, "My New Year's resolution is to get downstairs ten minutes earlier on school days!" She continued, "I am sure that my children will appreciate a happier mom and a more relaxing pace in the morning."

If I could have disappeared, I would have. *Wake up ten minutes earlier! Yes, this was truly the secret to world peace: begin with my own morning routine.* I went straight home and set my alarm clock to wake up ten minutes earlier. And it did transform my mornings. I used the first five minutes to meditate and get centered. When I walked downstairs, I felt calm and that naturally flowed onto my children. I used the other five minutes to leisurely greet my children. They responded immediately to the new and improved mom with more joy and a greater willingness to facilitate the morning's chores.

What will you do this week that takes ten minutes? Start small, and commit to something you know will nourish and energize you— something simple. Remember, I started with one practice: walking. At that time in my life, that was a big commitment. Only after months of walking did I add a second practice. Louise L. Hay, author of *You Can Heal Your Life,* says, "Be willing to take the first step, no matter how small it is. Concentrate on the fact that you are willing to learn. Absolute miracles will happen."

As you affirm your commitment to connect, take a moment to imagine the results. How do I feel as a result of connecting to myself? How do I feel as I relate to my family and friends from a place of connectedness? What's the emotional climate around me? Although the 239 Tinkertoys on the living room floor won't magically pick themselves up and fly back into the can, and you'll still have to call the plumber to extract Raggedy Ann's head from the toilet's depths, you'll do it with more peace and joy. And maybe even some laughter.

4. Return to Center Often

Connecting with yourself is an ongoing process, not something you do once a day. Our goal should be to live from a place of centeredness, and there are lots of reminders around us to do this, if we will take time to notice them.

I learned a valuable lesson about the importance of staying in balance one evening from a spider. I was saying goodnight to my dinner guests and as I stood at the back door, I noticed the moon illuminating a gigantic spider web in the upper corner of the doorway. We watched in awe as the mother spider set about capturing dinner, an array of gnats attracted by the porch light, for her and her babies. Her hunting practice was amazing. She sat poised in the middle of the web. When a gnat landed on the web, she shot out, snatched it up and bolted back to the center of the web. Over and over she caught the bugs and headed back to center. Never once did she go from one gnat to another without landing on home base first. What a lesson! Find center and return to it often. Don't go frantically from one side of your web to the other. From center, the distance to your goal is always shortest.

The more often you practice connecting to your center, the quicker you can get back to center when you find yourself in the middle of a parenting upset. The first step is to find center by practicing the Happy Mommy List. Then simply notice when you feel connected and when you don't.

I was reminded of the importance of often returning to center while listening to an audiotape on negotiating tips for buying a car. (Parenting tips do show up in the most interesting places if we are aware and centered!) The presenter, Roger Dawson, was telling the audience the importance of not buying under pressure. He said, "People under pressure become flexible." Flexible, as in easy to manipulate, and the car salesperson knows it! Isn't that true for us as parents? When we feel tired, frustrated, or rushed, the kids rule because we become unintentionally flexible. Most, if not all, parents have had the experience of saying a hasty, "yes" or "no" to a child when they were under pressure and regretted it later. A centered parent makes conscious decisions that are more likely to serve everyone in the long run.

5. Get Support

It's essential, when making life changes, to have the support of caring friends or family. You may want to partner up with a friend to support some of your self-care activities like walks or workouts or saying "no." Or perhaps check in once a week by phone or e-mail to report your progress. As an introvert, I know this alone can be a stretch for some people. I've had to step out of my comfort zone to ask for help.

It's fairly easy for most of us to ask for support when conditions become extreme, but we don't tend to ask for help in moving life from good to better. I wonder why that is. I know that when I was a child, I learned that to ask for help was a sign of weakness. Also, when I'm feeling negative I'm afraid I'll bring people down if I tell them what I'm going through.

After one of my children had been ill and home from school for ten days while I was on a writing deadline, I noticed one evening that I felt so stressed that at one point, I was unable to do one of my favorite centering techniques: taking three deep breaths. When I shared this with my friend Beth the following day, she ordered me to go to my yoga class. I realized my 11-year-old daughter was feeling better and could be alone for an hour or so and dragged myself there. For the first half of the class I fell over doing simple poses I'd done for years, I was that out of balance. By the end of the class, I *was* in balance, physically and emotionally. What a positive impact that had on the rest of my day. What a blessing to have a friend in my life—someone who understands what connects me and reminds me when I cannot see my options. Make sure your friends know what's on your Happy Mommy List, so they can remind you when you are blinded by overwhelm.

Many of us ask for help only when we're in extreme distress. It's almost as if we need *a really big reason* to justify reaching out. This pattern often comes from not feeling deserving, being addicted to high drama, or as I mentioned earlier, just being an introvert. Learn to ask for help when you notice you've become even somewhat disconnected with yourself. I found it helpful to monitor my need for support by regularly checking in and rating my state of mind on a continuum. I got in the habit of stopping a few times a day and asking, "Where am I on the connection continuum?" This practice helped me get better at asking for help before I approached extreme stress.

I think of a *Connection Continuum* like this:

The Connection Continuum

0———————————5———————————10

| Extreme Distress | Disconnected | Somewhat Disconnected | Connected | Bliss |

Make it a goal to monitor your stress level and ask for support when you get to the "somewhat disconnected" level. Here is some of the damaging self-talk that keeps us from asking for help or only asking when we are approaching extreme distress:

Discouraging Self-Talk (first thought)	Encouraging Self-Talk (second thought)
"I'm fine, really . . . I can handle this."	"I might want to call for help before I get too stressed."
"I'll feel like such a failure if I ask for help."	"I am a wonderful parent doing the best I can do."
"I don't want to bother anyone."	"People really enjoy helping others. I'll let others be responsible for setting their boundaries."

REACHING OUT, BIT BY BIT

When I began learning about self-care, asking for support was wildly out of my comfort zone. Like a person getting on a bike for the first time, it felt and looked awkward. For me, it began with asking my husband. His whole purpose in life seems to be to encourage and support people, so it felt safe to start with him. Start with your most supportive family member or friend. Here's how my asking has evolved:

HOW I LEARNED TO ASK FOR HELP SOONER

	My Connection Continuum Rating	The Words I Used	My Tone of Voice	My Result
In the Early Days	Extreme Distress	I either said nothing and allowed the resentments to build up or I said, "I'm sick and tired of no one caring about my needs. I'm going on a walk right now. You can fix dinner!"	Angry, demanding, controlling, and extremely attached to the outcome.	Strain between my husband and me that inevitably flowed over onto the children.
As I Learned More	Disconnected	"I really, really, really need some time alone. Could you watch the kids?"	Frustrated.	Less strain in the family. Hope for relief.
Today	Somewhat Disconnected-Connected	"I have a busy speaking schedule next month. I would really appreciate your support in this way . . ."	Detached and calm. A tone of positive expectation.	I feel connected to my husband and children.

Still having a hard time finding the words and tone of voice to use when asking for support? Try saying this: "Honey, the car needs an oil change. It's been 3,000 miles since the last one." What tone of voice would you use to make that communication? Probably detached, expectant, and calm. You would fully expect support from your partner to schedule and pay for required maintenance on a vehicle. Do you have the same positive communication style when you discuss your needs? If not, practice with a trusted friend until you do. Your family will reap the rewards of having a peaceful parent.

50 WAYS TO CALM YOUR MOTHER (OR FATHER)

When you feel disconnected from your center, experiment with one of the following practices. Here are 50 ideas for getting back to center, in order of the amount of time required.

Back to Center Practices

When you have 30 seconds to reconnect:

- Take three deep breaths (see Chapter Three)

When you have one minute to reconnect:

- Take ten whole-body breaths
- Do ten jumping jacks
- Do a headstand (yoga practice for dramatic shift in consciousness)
- Watch a sunrise or sunset
- Dance
- Sit in silence
- Do nothing

When you have five to ten minutes to reconnect, take three deep breaths and choose one or more of the following:

- Journal

- Pound on a drum

- Take a short walk

- Write an encouraging note to someone

- Drink 16 oz. of water

- Read something inspirational

- Call an encouraging friend

When you have 30 minutes to reconnect, take three deep breaths and choose one or more of the following:

- Listen to a guided meditation

- Dance

- Throw a ball

- Take a walk

- Take a catnap

- Enjoy a quiet cup of tea

- Do some meditative household task like organizing a drawer or matching socks

When you have one hour to reconnect:

- Take a bath

- Call a friend for a catch-up chat

- Connect with nature

- Spend time with your pet

- Give yourself a pedicure

- Take a nap

- Exercise

When you have a full day to reconnect:

- Take a day trip
- Take a day hike
- Go shopping and to lunch
- Turn off the phone and computer and get lost in a good book
- Spend a day at home puttering
- Go to a spa
- Attend a workshop

When you have a weekend to reconnect:

- Attend a weekend workshop
- Go away with your significant other or a close friend
- Attend a silent meditation retreat
- Spend a weekend with yourself, doing what you love most
- Spend a weekend with yourself on a home improvement project
- Plan and plant a garden
- Pick a place on the map you haven't visited and go explore

What else would you add to this list? You may want to make a copy and keep it handy for those moments when things suddenly seem to go out of control.

You may have noticed that a lot of these suggestions are downright fun. You have both my permission and my encouragement to enjoy life. It's one of the greatest gifts you can give your child. In fact, according to Talmud Yerushalmi, "We will be held accountable for all the permitted pleasures we failed to enjoy." Don't you just love that?

Prayer/Affirmation

That which nourishes, heals, and strengthens me
also nourishes, heals, and strengthens my family.

Soulful Reminders

- **Give yourself permission to take care of yourself.**

- **Find center and discover what connects you.**

- **Return to center often.**

- **Start small. Remember even five to ten minutes a day
  of self-care can dramatically impact your family.**

- **Get support.**

The Power of One Small Step

Write down one practice you learned or were reminded of in
this chapter that you will use this week to better connect with yourself. I started by setting my alarm ten minutes earlier and using that
time to get centered.

2

create your parenting vision

If there is light in the soul,
there will be beauty in the person.
If there is beauty in the person,
there will be harmony in the house.
If there is harmony in the house,
there will be order in the nation.
If there is order in the nation,
there will be peace in the world.

— LAO-TZU,
CHINESE MYSTIC

Once you've connected with yourself, connect with your dream. What's your highest vision of yourself as a parent? To be loving, understanding, and wise? Do you long for connection, yet meet with disappointment instead? Over the past ten years offering parenting classes to thousands of parents and caregivers, I've learned a great truth: *We all want the same things:*

- **A close, connected relationship with our children.**

- **Joyful interactions with our family.**

- **Children who feel capable, happy, and self-confident.**

- **To parent as a loving, supportive team with our partner or spouse.**

- **Feeling good about so much of the way we parent.**

Within us are all the answers we need to create a joyful parenting experience. We are powerful creators and we can learn to work in harmony with the laws of the universe to tap into our vast stores of inner wisdom. An

27

understanding of how the universe works is all that's required to create the parenting experience we long for.

FAST FORWARD

If you're like me, you often parent with only short-term goals in mind: to get the kids to clean their rooms, to make it through the grocery store without buying a toy, or to induce them to sit quietly through church or temple. It's easy to lose sight of our long-term goals of raising happy, healthy, confident children when we are caught up in the minutia of life. I find that for most parents in my programs, it is helpful to be powerfully reminded of the end result of your minute-to-minute decisions. So I developed a visualization called *Fast Forward* to help parents create a picture that they carry with them through the six-week parenting course and beyond. Please read the exercise and then take the time to write down your response that follows the visualization, immediately and without editing, your first thoughts.

Fast Forward your life to a future scene. Your child, now 19, has just arrived home from college to join you for Thanksgiving (if you have more than one child, picture the child who challenges you the most). As you take your seat among friends and family at the dinner table, your 19-year-old clinks a glass to get everyone's attention, stands and begins to give a speech in your honor. You feel *overwhelmed* with the feelings of connectedness, joy, and pride as you hear your child express his/her deep gratitude for the wonderful parent you have been.

On a piece of paper write your child's speech—the speech you would like to hear. Be as specific as possible, listing in detail the circumstances that created closeness between you and your child. Let your imagination go wild. Do not limit yourself by what you *think* is possible—write the dream.

This can be a very emotional experience for most parents. Many of us as children did not receive from our parents what we really want to pass on to our children—a high level of connection, appreciation, and unconditional love. Also, many parents fear they won't be able to "get it" in time to become the parents they want to be. You will. It's never ever too late to become a more effective parent. It's never too late to create a more connected relationship with your child.

Use this exercise as a way to set your intention for how you want to raise your children, and let this bigger intention guide your daily actions and provide you with the motivation to change. You provide the desire and I will provide you plenty of ideas for getting there. If you feel like you did not receive the qualities that you want to pass on to your children, do not despair. One of the grand possibilities of parenthood is that we have the chance to experience gifts like unconditional love, connection, freedom, and being heard when we give them to our child. We get to experience unconditional love by giving it to someone else. We have an opportunity to create the connection we didn't feel as children when we connect with our child. And we experience the joy of hearing someone when we felt unheard. In the process we all get to heal.

FOUR SOUL TOOLS

Before we begin this journey, let me give you four tools that will help each of the principles in this book become second nature:

1. New Self-Talk

Perhaps the most important determining factor in our success as a parent is our ability to shape the conversations we have with ourselves. Our beliefs, both conscious and unconscious, flavor our day-to-day experiences in ways we may not even be aware of. These beliefs show up in our self-talk.

We inherit our beliefs and self-talk from our parents, teachers, peers, and society at large. Some of our beliefs serve us. I call these *encouraging* beliefs. Some of our beliefs prevent us from realizing our desires, be it for more closeness, health, or money— I call these *discouraging* beliefs.

A belief is simply a thought you keep thinking over and over. One of the most radical and helpful changes I have made to improve my parenting is monitoring and (over time) changing my self-talk. We can begin to change our beliefs by simply inserting a new encouraging thought in place of the old or discouraging one. Simple, yes. Easy, no. It will take a strong desire to change your beliefs. It starts with noticing your self-talk. Then, choose a second thought that's more encouraging than the first one. Eventually, you will automatically choose a more uplifting thought.

Getting to this stage takes years, so for now, know that just adding a more encouraging second thought greatly increases your joy and effectiveness as a parent.

Here is an example of the Self-Talk charts you will see throughout the book:

Discouraging Self-Talk (first thought)	Encouraging Self-Talk (second thought)
"I'll never be able to figure out all this self-talk stuff. It's too hard."	"I'm willing to experiment with this to see if I notice any improvement."

2. New Language

The exact words you use powerfully shape your relationships. Along with your tone, your words form the landscape of your parenting experience. You may find it helpful to have some *New Language* suggestions that support your new objectives.

Much of the common language used in our culture limits our ability to grow into a more conscious parent. Very few of us lived in homes where effective language was used. On the next page is an example of the New Language charts that you will see throughout the book:

Limiting Language	Expansive Language
"You never offer to watch the kids so I can go do something for myself!" (The other extreme) "I'm fine here with the kids, honey [when you're not]. You go ahead and go visit your mother this weekend."	(In a detached tone of voice) "John, I would really like to have about an hour to read my book. Would you mind taking the kids to the park?"

3. The Power of One Small Step

I've seen many a parent exit the first night of the six-week parenting class with a long list of "to do's" they've created, only to return the next week exasperated and discouraged by their "failures."

"I'm going to encourage my child, take time for myself, improve my communication with my spouse, and abolish sibling rivalry this week," they say gleefully as they skip out of the room. In their excitement to transform, they take on the impossible task of what I call "just add water" personal growth. However, they sadly find that, just like anything else, developing a new parenting practice takes time—just add practice.

To head off this kind of discouragement, it's important to embrace the idea of "The Power of One Small Step." At the end of each class, each parent chooses only one new practice, from the many discussed each night, to try at home the following week. When parents commit to only one practice, their chances of succeeding skyrocket and with that success comes the self-confidence and courage to grow even more. It can seem boring to work on *only* one practice and may feel tempting to change mid-week, but your success depends on your commitment to go slowly. At the end of each chapter, you have the opportunity to choose one idea from the chapter, write it down and practice it for one week. If you will participate in the "power of one small step," you will succeed.

4. Weekly Prayer/Affirmation

When we're changing, it helps to have a prayer, affirmation, or mantra of some kind to repeat each day to help us stay focused. I suggest you spend a week on each chapter and use the prayer I've suggested or another one of your choosing everyday to keep the idea in your consciousness. Have fun with this. Be outrageous. Make it long, short, or a single word. This practice will speed your change along.

So we start down the path together. I bow to you for the love you feel for your child and for the courage to parent with soul.

Prayer/Affirmation

I bless the parents I have had,
who did their best,
and I give thanks
for the parent I will become.

Soulful Reminders

- **It's never too late to create a more connected relationship with your child.**

- **Allow your future vision of your child to guide your daily actions and provide you with the motivation to change.**

- **Commit to changing only one practice per week and greatly increase your chances for success.**

The Power of One Small Step

Begin your Parenting with Soul journey by completing a simple but powerful exercise to raise your own level of awareness right now. Take a breath. Now thoughtfully fill in the answer to the following statement:

My one intention for reading this book is to:

_____ .

When you take just a moment to pause and ask yourself, "What do I want in this situation?" you support the universe in granting your desires. Too often we jump into circumstances unclear about exactly what we want. Our lack of clarity is the reason we waste time and don't get what we want out of life. When we get clear, whether about our life goal or what our child can eat for lunch, we greatly increase our chances of attracting what we long for. Consciously setting your intention for reading this book will greatly increase your chances of becoming the parent you hope to be.

How did you fill in the blank? If you haven't already, I suggest you take the time to complete the statement. By doing this, you announce to the universe, "I am ready to learn and grow."

3

breathe!

You only need
to breathe consciously
one or two times
and you will recover
your smile.

— THICH NHAT HANH

The way we connect our dream with reality is to breathe. Marsha, a mother of two, glances at the clock and realizes it's already 7:22 A.M. She notices her temperature rise and her chest constrict as she realizes that once again the kids are running late for the bus. She feels the pressure of a "no-win" situation, not able to drive the kids to school that morning because she has an important conference call. Her frustration builds. "How can I get these kids out of here on time? Why won't they move faster?" Marsha loves her children. She just doesn't know what else to try at this point, except what she's always done.

She barks rapid-fire commands in a booming voice, "Get your coats on! Hurry up!" Her six-year-old starts to cry, the nine-year-old flashes her an angry look. The kids have to run the entire four blocks to the bus stop, gasping for breath as they just make it, but it takes them more than an hour to start feeling better. Sadness and disappointment with herself play like low-level background music all day for their mom.

A few doors down, Pam finds herself in the same situation. The kids are running late and it looks like they may not make the bus. She, too, has an important phone appointment and can't drive them to school. She feels her temperature rise and her chest constrict. Her frustration builds. She quickly recognizes this as her signal that she has disconnected. "How can I connect and bring more peace to this morning (and have the kids make the bus)?" she asks herself. She takes three deep breaths as she remembers the words of her yoga instructor, "The fastest way to get back to center is through the breath."

Feeling a little more centered, she connects with an idea: "I'll drive them to the bus stop. It's only four blocks away; that way we can save a couple of minutes of walking time and I'll still make my appointment." She takes a few more deep breaths. As calmly as she can, she says, "Hey, I have an idea. I'll drive you to the bus stop, so don't worry about missing the bus. What else do you need for today? We need to leave in two minutes." They arrive at the bus stop one minute early. Pam uses the minute to make loving eye contact with both her girls and gives them a positive send-off. She's still breathing deeply. She arrives back home in plenty of time for her call, feeling great.

Pam has solved a parenting challenge from a powerfully centered place.

Everyone feels much better, and the joy of the positive resolution flavors their whole day. Pam feels elated at the power of the simple breathing practices she's been putting to use for the past few months since discovering the power of Parenting with Soul.

How did Pam transform a negative situation into one of calm and connection while Marsha struggled? Pam had discovered the power of the breath to change her mental state. Marsha has yet to learn the benefits of breathwork.

I have been Pam and I have been Marsha. In fact, these two stories are me "before" and "after" learning how to breathe my way through parenting. My devotion and commitment to the practice of conscious breathing has transformed many of my parenting experiences from frustration to peaceful resolution. As I slowly and steadily become better at dealing with parenting ups and downs this way, life gets calmer. It will for you, too.

Parents who use conscious breathing can change the course of many sticky situations (both literally and figuratively!). Simply willing ourselves to change is often not enough, especially in the heat of the moment. Andrew Weil, M.D., the author of *8 Weeks to Optimum Health,* validated this point when he said, "If you are upset, you can't always just tell yourself to settle down, but you can always change your breathing in the direction of making it deeper, slower, quieter, and more regular. By doing so, you affect your physiology, both the body response and the mental state."

One of the many benefits of taking three deep breaths is that it creates a space for us to choose a more uplifting and effective second thought. Over time, my self-talk has changed and my responses have become more effective. Here's how I've changed, thanks to breathing:

Discouraging Self-Talk (first thought)	Encouraging Self-Talk (second thought)
"Those kids have to get on that bus or I'll be very upset!" (Attached) "What's wrong with you that you can't complete the simple task of getting your kids to the bus on time?" (Judging)	""How can I get centered and creative fast?" (Breathe) "My negativity will ruin this. How can I set a positive tone?" (Breathe) "If I get attached, this whole situation will tank. I need to let it go." (Breathe)

Parents who've taken my Parenting with Soul course have shared similar experiences. They often report that the *single most helpful practice* they learned in the entire six weeks was also the simplest: *conscious breathing.*

- **Instead of yelling, they breathe.**

- **Instead of worrying, they breathe.**

- **Instead of becoming upset, they breathe.**

- **Instead of regretting the past, they breathe.**

- **Instead of becoming anxious about the future, they breathe.**

- **Instead of responding with angry, cynical, or controlling words, they breathe.**

And their relationships with their children have been transformed. How can such an elementary practice create such profound results? Jack Downing, M.D., a pioneer of body-centered therapy, postulated more than 30 years ago that if everyone took an hour a day to breathe and to do creative movement, there would be little need for mental health facilities. Need I say more?

Breathing is a form of prayer in many spiritual movements. Many types of meditation focus on the breath, and the Buddhist practice of Tonglen links breathing with healing the world. In this practice, you simply breathe in your own or someone else's pain or anger and breathe out peace and love. With each breath, inhale the pain, then exhale love. You do not need to worry whether you are doing it "right." Just set your intention as you take each breath. According to the Buddhists, you can even focus on breathing in the pain of all beings and breathing out peace. You will be healing yourself and all others at the same time. For most of us, though, our only encounter with conscious breathing has been in the birthing room.

LAMAZE BEYOND
THE BIRTHING ROOM

Like many expectant parents, my husband and I enrolled in Lamaze childbirth classes when we were expecting our first child. The various relaxation techniques and breathing exercises worked beautifully, and I delivered her (and three years later, her sister) naturally, without anesthesia.

Then, just when I thought I had left Lamaze in the delivery room, I was reminded of the power of conscious breathing when my daughter was six weeks old and I broke my leg skiing. I instinctively went back to the deep breathing to manage the pain while on the mountain and later in the hospital. I was nursing and didn't want to use drugs, and I got through the whole 12-week healing cycle without them. I found, and I think you will too, that breathing is just as useful (some parents would say even more so) *after* labor as during.

Our most essential and powerful parenting tool is always available, doesn't cost a thing, and was one of our primary talents. In fact, it was the first thing we did after we were born.

Take a deep breath right now.

When we pause to take three (or more) deep breaths, several miracles occur. Here's a sampling:

1. We Step Into the Present Moment

The act of taking three deep breaths is possibly the most transformative of all the connecting practices because of its simplicity and instant results. In most situations, three deep breaths bring us back into the moment, back into our bodies, back to center. We become present, more able to accurately assess situations and make sound decisions.

Have you ever been so busy or distracted that you didn't notice you'd somehow injured yourself and were bruised or bleeding? Have you ever felt as if so much information was coming at you that you couldn't think straight? We're moving so fast, so much of the time that we barely know what we're feeling, physically or emotionally. The stresses and pace of life today often disconnect us from ourselves.

I experienced one of my most disconnected moments several years ago at an outdoor concert with my husband and four toddlers. I had spent hours frantically running after the children, and suddenly realized our 18-month-old was missing. I approached my husband and worriedly asked, "Where's Alexa?" He looked at me in disbelief then answered, *"She's in your backpack."*

If I had taken the time to breathe when I first thought Alexa was missing, I might have gotten present enough to feel that precious 20 pound weight on my back instead of going unconscious and increasing my anxious exhaustion by searching for the child who was with me all the time.

Stressful parenting situations can easily take us out of the present moment and leave us feeling overwhelmed, upset, or afraid. The present moment is the only place where we have an opportunity to make a positive difference. Breathing brings us back there.

2. We "Buy Time" and Create Space for More Creative and Effective Parenting Ideas to Emerge

When we take three deep breaths, we inject about 30 seconds of silence into a situation, preventing us from talking too much, yelling, or even hitting—our least effective parenting tools. Students in my parenting classes often ask, "What should I do when my child hits his brother, screams at me in the grocery store, bites, etc.?" I always tell them, "First, breathe." The Dalai Lama reminds us that, "When human emotions come out of control, then the best part of the brain in which we make judgments cannot function properly." What we often do first in tense situations is talk, and words are like fuel. Adding fuel to a fiery situation just stokes the fire.

IN AN EMERGENCY, REMEMBER THESE FORMULAS
Words = Fuel   **Upset + Words = More Upset**   **Upset + Conscious Breathing = More Calm**

I agree with the TV public service announcements that say simply: "Count to ten instead of hitting your child." These people know the power of injecting just a few short moments of nonaction into a tense situation. If you breathe while you count, the resulting relaxation increases your chances for success even more.

One of my coaching clients shared a success story that illustrates the power of this practice:

I first tried taking three deep breaths to deal with my struggle with my eight-year-old son Brian about brushing his teeth. When we ask him to brush his teeth, he launches into a big long story about his day or one of his friends or what he saw on TV to create a diversion. I have a quick temper, so I get angry and frustrated and yell at him. Then we both feel terrible and he refuses to tell me the story he started.

One night, I decided to try taking three deep breaths. I asked him to brush his teeth and sure enough, he started with the story. I breathed deeply instead of reacting in my usual way. I did feel calmer than usual and calmer words came. I said, "Brian, I would like to hear your story after you brush your teeth." In the past, I would scream, "I don't want to hear it! Just brush your teeth!"

Since I had not hurt his feelings by screaming, he told me his story later and we got to really connect.

*Taking three deep breaths gives me a moment to decide
to respond in a better way, and it helps me be patient—
something that's very hard for me.*

P.S. It also works with my husband.

3. We Slow Our Respiration and Instantly Reduce the Anxiety Created by the Automatic "Fight or Flight" Response

I had a chance to breathe on a grand scale during a family vacation a few years ago. My husband comes from a big New York Italian clan, and one summer, all 18 of us traveled to Disneyworld together. My in-laws are among the most loving people I know, as well as the most animated and loud. There are also lots of "chiefs," and the assertiveness, the noise levels, and the waving of hands when we get together are way beyond anything I'm used to.

I wondered how I could take care of myself during this vacation. When the noise level got to be too much for me on previous visits, I often felt overwhelmed and would check out mentally or literally walk away to regroup. My goal was to stay centered amidst the chaos, so I decided to do it differently this time. I decided to breathe in a big way.

A few days before we left, I told my family that whenever things became heated in the Magic Kingdom, I'd perform a little magic of my own. I was going to close my eyes, touch thumbs and index fingers in a meditative pose and begin to chant, "Om." We weren't five feet inside Disneyworld when I had my first opportunity.

"Come on! Let's take the kids to Fantasyland!"

"No! We've got to ride the Tower of Terror. It's the best ride, and it's on the other side of the park!"

"Are you nuts? We need to eat now so we don't get caught up in the lunch lines!"

I began to "om."

My girls giggled, and my husband looked the other way. The cacophony of strong opinions ceased as the other family members stared in a mix of amazement, confusion, and embarrassment.

"What are you doing?"

"She's acting *crazy*."

"For God's sake," my mother-in-law said to me. "I'm a city councilwoman!"

My children gleefully took on the role of tour guides in a foreign land, interpreting this strange custom: "That's what Mom does when she gets upset."

During our five-day trip, I "omed" an average of once a day when things hit a crescendo; I "omed" instead of losing it. Every time I did, it changed the energy of the group, often because they stopped shouting and started laughing. One time, an incipient "discussion" about where to sit in the Nine Dragons Chinese restaurant came to an abrupt halt, as one relative looked over and said, "Okay. We'll get a table. Just don't 'om.'" I still cherish the photo one of them took of me "oming" in the gardens of the Epcot Center.

I was not breathing deeply to amuse everyone. Not in the beginning, anyway. I was sincerely trying to change my state. But my "antics" had served to lighten up the whole crew. Who knows? It *could* happen to you. Such is the power of breathing. It's free. It's portable. It's extraordinarily effective. *Breathe!*

4. We Begin to Diffuse the Intense and Destructive Emotions of Fear and Anger— Our Children's and Our Own

The biggest challenge of my parenting career, bar none, is sibling rivalry. The agony of watching someone I love and adore deliberately harm another whom I love and adore is almost always too much to bear. It seems ironic that this is also the area where I have experienced the most success—and breathing played an important role.

One of the parenting tools Kathryn Kvols teaches in *Redirecting Children's Behavior* is called "bring peace to the fight." This practice encourages parents to arrive at the scene of a fight with an air of peace and calm instead of the typical anger and frustration that is sure to escalate things. This practice worked beautifully for me—in theory.

In the early years, I didn't quite know where to find the peace to bring to the fight. I believed in the practice. But when the angry words started to fly, the peaceful mommy who taught the parenting class the previous night was nowhere in sight!

Over the years, I discovered two reservoirs of peace. One was my self-care practice. When I nurtured and connected with myself, I had more peace to bring to the fight or any intense situation. The other discovery was the power of the breath. So when the fights broke out, I would instantly start breathing deeply. The breathing centered me and I was able to "bring peace to the fight" because I had found some for myself. You will too, if you create your own reservoirs.

BREATHING: NOT JUST FOR PARENTS

Anger is not the only negative emotion we can diffuse with breathing. By modeling and teaching proper breathing, we give children a meaningful tool to manage fear and pain also.

We were vacationing with another family and had hired a babysitter to watch the kids at the hotel while the adults went to dinner. When I arrived at the hotel after dinner, I was greeted by a frantic man asking, "Is anyone in this taxi William's mom?" My heart sank. "I'm his mother's friend and she's ten minutes behind us," I said. "What's wrong?" "He's hurt. Come here." William was in the lobby rocking back and forth crying hysterically while the babysitter held a blood-soaked bandage on his badly injured finger.

"Where's my mom?" the nine-year-old wailed. I could feel my heart pound, my chest constrict, and my blood pressure rise as I assessed the situation. I started breathing deeply. In less than a minute, I was feeling much calmer. After a few minutes of just sitting with him, I asked him if he could take a deep breath.

"*Noooooo!*" he replied. "I'm afraid. I just want my mom!" "It will help with the pain," I said calmly. "Put your hand on your belly and breathe down there." "I can't. I can't I can't," he sobbed. Yet he seemed to want to, so I gently coached him and he finally took one deep breath. I stayed peaceful and detached. (More about detachment in Chapter Eleven: Attract What You Want.) If he had asked me to stop or leave at any time, I would have.

He continued to breathe deeply for a few minutes. By the time his mother arrived, he had radically shifted his energy and was feeling less anxious and afraid.

Gay Hendricks, Ph.D., in his book *Conscious Breathing,* talks about the power of breathing to dissipate negative feelings like anger and fear. He demonstrates how to do this without either denying the feeling or letting the feeling overtake us: "Once you get the message from a feeling [say, 'I'm scared'], you may want to make it disappear. Breathing is the fastest and most effective way to do this. Take a few big breaths into the physical sensations of any emotion, and watch what happens. Many times, that's all it takes to move it out of your body."

5. We Stop the Forward Momentum Toward Chaos

Heed the advice of Roman philosopher Seneca: "Hesitation is the best cure for anger . . . the first blows of anger are heavy, but if it waits, it will think again."

Breathing reconnects us to our center and increases our chances for effective parenting. We also model for our children a powerful way to deal with negative situations, and we may change the energy of a situation just by providing a reason for our children to laugh at us. On more than one occasion, I've done exactly that.

My husband and I had scheduled a date one autumn evening and I was running late. As I walked in from picking up the sitter, I could feel my husband's anger. He wanted to leave on time. I felt upset about his upset, the sitter felt flustered, and to top it off, my children were in the den fighting loudly over possession of the remote control. Very intense!

I walked over to the dining room table and the sitter, a close friend, followed sheepishly. I put my hand on the table, closed my eyes and began to take several slow, deep breaths. When I opened my eyes, the sitter was nearly nose-to-nose with me. "Vickie, what *are* you doing?" she asked. I closed my eyes and continued with my deep breaths. "Girls, come here! What *is* your mom doing?" she called to the next room. My girls dropped the remote and came running. They laughed out loud. "Oh that's what my mom does when she gets stressed out—she takes three deep breaths!" The sitter giggled, my kids roared, and my husband joined in. I had diffused the entire situation. My intention was not to amuse everyone. My intention was simply to calm down. I had also stopped the forward momentum toward chaos and changed the tone of the entire family.

6. We Model Peace

When my older child was seven, she did a flip off the side of a pool and hit her head on the edge, cutting her head to the skull. The moment I realized what had happened, I began breathing deeply so I could be completely present for her and so my calmness could help her stay calm. Three hours later, as we headed home from the emergency room, the nurses remarked that I had been the calmest mother they'd ever seen. And all I did was breathe deeply the whole time. Three years later when my younger child sustained an even more serious injury, cutting her ear in half playing whirling dervishes in the living room (she whirled out of orbit into the fireplace), I was an even better breather. In both cases, my calm state really helped my girls get through a tough experience.

In his audiotape, *Breathing: The Master Key to Self Healing*, Andrew Weil, M.D., points out that when we feel angry, frustrated, or afraid, invariably our breathing pattern is rapid, shallow, irregular, and noisy. We can move toward harmony and reduce stress by consciously making our breathing pattern deep, slow, quiet, and regular. He promotes breathwork as a way to control anxiety, regulate moods, help people relax, and improve general health. "There's no single more powerful—or more simple—daily practice to further your health and well-being than breathwork," according to Weil.

Chaos happens. The resulting effect of the chaos is in our hands, or rather in our lungs.

THE ART OF THE BREATH

As babies, we did it right, using our whole bodies, breathing all the way in and all the way out. Observe any infant and you'll see the rise and fall of her diaphragm as she takes a full-body, natural breath. Primitive cultures that were more in tune with the natural rhythms of life breathed deeply into the abdomen and only shifted into fight-or-flight chest breathing when confronting a dangerous situation. With civilization came more stress, and now most people breathe routinely from their chests, in shallow spurts that starve the body, mind, and spirit.

Gay Hendricks, Ph.D., says, "If you can learn to breathe even a little bit better, you will notice immediate, profound shifts in your physical, mental, and emotional well-being." Whole-body breathing dramatically releases stress and tension in day-to-day parenting challenges. It's free, easy, and effective.

Take air in as far down in your belly as you can imagine. Visualize your body filling up. If you don't already breathe with your whole body, this may feel awkward at first, but as with all new skills, practice makes a difference. Many people find it hard to take a really deep breath. If that's true for you, start with exhalation. Breathe all the way out, pulling your stomach in to force out the last bit of air. It's much easier for most of us to begin the breathing cycle with exhalation because our exhaling muscles (abdominals and diaphragm) are much stronger than the muscles we use to inhale.

Here are some exercises that promote whole-body breathing:

Rocking Breaths

- **Lie on your back on the floor, on a firm sofa, or bed. You may bend your knees if that feels more comfortable.**

- Place one hand on your diaphragm and one hand on your chest so that you can monitor your airflow. Begin by fully exhaling.

- Slowly take a deep breath, inhaling as deeply into your belly as you can imagine, tilting your tailbone toward your feet and arching your back, as your stomach expands.

- As you slowly exhale, tilt your pelvis toward your chin, as your lungs empty and your diaphragm collapses inward.

- Empty your chest first, then your diaphragm.

Sitting Breaths

These are similar to rocking breaths, but in an upright position. You may practice in a desk chair or a straight back chair.

- Sit comfortably in a chair with your feet on the floor.

- While slowly taking in a deep breath, notice yourself leaning back as your back arches and your stomach expands.

- As you slowly exhale, tighten the muscles of your stomach to expel all the air and notice yourself leaning slightly forward.

If you do five to ten of either of these exercises each day, you will train your body to take more whole breaths. For more ideas, check out **www.hendricks.com** and **www.dailybreath.com**. You'll find other helpful resources about whole-body breathing in the Resources section at the end of this book.

WHEN SHOULD YOU BREATHE?

I have one friend who took the whole breathing thing so seriously that she bought a video and practiced breathing exercises for a year. (Need I say she didn't have small children at home?) And she did change her breathing pattern. Most of us don't have time for one more thing in our day, but we do have lots of moments when we can practice whole-body breathing, one breath at a time. Here are some possibilities:

- **Waiting for your bath or shower water to warm up**

- **At red lights and stop signs (stop and breathe)**

- **Waiting for your computer to download a program or large file**

- **Standing in line in stores**

- **Filling your car with gas (first, step away from the harmful fumes)**

- **Waiting on hold**

- **Before a meal**

Take one whole-body breath right now and pay attention to the entire process—inhalation, the way your stomach then lungs expand, the way they contract as you breathe it all out. Over time, you'll notice yourself breathing in this whole-body way more and more often.

BREATHING INTO YOUR DAY

Sometimes it's helpful to think ahead about the times when we most need to breathe and might not remember to. Picture the following situations and add some of your own:

- **You're due to make a big presentation at work and the school nurse calls to say your child has a fever of 103° F and needs to go home**

- **You walk into a room that's in shambles after an afternoon of fort building**

- **When involved in some dramatic conversation, instead of saying, "Oh, my God!"**

- **When your child has been injured**

- **When your child is late returning home**

- **Whenever you don't know what to say**

- **Whenever life throws you a curveball**

- **When life is good and you're willing for it to become even better**

- **For no particular reason**

- **Right now**

BREATHING INTO THE NEXT GENERATION

Several years ago I conducted a daylong training for the local branch of the National Association for the Education of Young Children (NAEYC). A week later I received an e-mail from Tracy, one of the preschool teachers at the training. She shared the power of breathing, even for young children. At the end of the workshop, Tracy had chosen to practice a skill other than three deep breaths during the following week. But she realized the first day back in the classroom that, Mira, a 22-month-old girl, who "lost it" regularly, might benefit from learning to take three deep breaths.

One day after an upset, Tracy showed Mira how to breathe by making her tummy big and then reminded her by saying, "breathe," whenever the girl's emotions started to flare. Tracy would also take a deep breath herself and exhale slowly to model. A week later the child's delighted mother said she'd observed her daughter breathing through her nose and exhaling out her mouth instead of screaming when she felt frustrated. "Wow! Did you teach her this? Thank you!"

I had never talked about using this with children and felt ecstatic to hear of this huge success with such a young child. When we adopt the conscious breathing practices many of us left in the birthing room as a way of life, we reap the benefits in all parts of our lives. And many others do as well.

Prayer/Affirmation

- I breathe in disharmony and I breathe out peace.

- I breathe in sadness and I breathe out joy.

- I breathe in woundedness and breathe out healing.

- I breathe in hatred and breathe out compassion.

- I breathe in fear and I breathe out love.

Soulful Reminders

- **Three deep breaths bring us back into connection with ourselves and bring more peace and calm.**

- **Conscious breathing is simple and brings instant results.**

- **When we take three deep breaths, we bring peace to stressful situations. Talking often adds fuel to the fire.**

- **When we breathe consciously, we model for our children a powerful way to deal with negative situations.**

- **Take air in as far down in your belly as you can imagine.**

- **Make space in your day during ordinary activities, like stopping for a red light, for whole-body breathing.**

- **Teach your children how to breathe when they become upset or injured.**

THE POWER OF ONE

Write down one practice you learned or were reminded of in this chapter that you will use this week to remember to breathe. I started by using the Lamaze exercises I'd learned on my broken leg to manage the pain. Later, I breathed deeply anytime I became upset.

4

the change process

To change your life:
start immediately;
do it flamboyantly,
no exceptions.

— WILLIAM JAMES

At this point, with so many changes in your parenting, the most helpful connection you can make is with the Change Process itself. I always loved the fourth evening of the six-week parenting class I taught in the nineties. After a month of success with new practices, the parents were glowing. The breakthroughs were happening. The peace and joy were palpable.

One night, however, was different.

It was a cold October evening, and after a few of the parents had shared their achievements with the group, a hand shot up in the front row. "I don't know what these people are talking about, because my life has never been so miserable," said the mother of three. "It seems like since I started this class, I'm an even worse mother than I was before coming here!"

My face burned red. I had been ready to serenely accept everyone's appreciation and thanks, and this woman seemed to wax on endlessly about the misery I had caused her by teaching skills that were "unattainable." I didn't know what to say. I stumbled and mumbled and moved quickly to the next exercise.

That was *before* I understood the change process. Luckily, I came across the work of William Howell, a communication researcher at the University of Minnesota, shortly after that. In subsequent classes, I introduced the information I'll be sharing with you about changing behaviors on the first night of class. Invariably, sighs of relief would fill the room as parents heard, often for the first time, the natural progression of the change process. They realized they not only wouldn't but couldn't parent with soul overnight.

FLABBY THIGHS
AND PARENTING WITH SOUL

Sometimes it helps to look at some area other than parenting to more objectively appreciate the approach many of us take in modifying ourselves and our lives. My friend Shawna is a personal trainer who works with moms, athletes, and Hollywood stars to help them get fit. Here is her recurring frustration: A woman shows up for her first session wanting to have thin, cellulite-free thighs for her 20th high school reunion in six weeks.

When Shawna introduces the exercise program, including weight training, diet improvements, and cardiovascular training, the woman becomes frustrated. Nearly every suggestion is met with, "Yes, but, how will this help me get thin thighs?" Shawna tries to explain that the cumulative effect of the program is all-over muscle tone, more energy, and less body fat, which includes the thighs.

But the woman insists, "More exercises for my thighs! I don't want to hear about veggies and jogging and bicep curls. It's my *thighs* that need help!" Shawna laments, "Some people just don't get that it's the total program that gets results, not spot-training. They fail to see that it's a lifestyle, not something you do for six weeks so you can fit into your new black dress."

Parents often arrive at seminars and coaching sessions wanting similar spot-training. How do I get Curtis to eat dinner? How can I motivate Samantha to get dressed in the morning? They want to know how to get their kids to listen to them, stop fighting, clean their rooms, do their homework, and take out the garbage while whistling "Dixie." Or, at least, not slam the door on their way out.

Like Shawna's fitness clients, some parents feel less interested in adopting lifelong practices than in learning tools. "Tools, yes! That's what we need, more tools to get our children to behave!" So I give them tools. And woven in between the tips and techniques are the "practices," the ways of being with your child that foster close long-term relationships and ultimately a successful parenting experience. Accepting the change process is one of these practices.

THE CHANGE PROCESS: LET 'ER RIP!

If you've ever had arthroscopic knee surgery, you may have experienced the essential and excruciating physical therapy that follows to break the adhesions that form while the knee is immobilized following surgery. Many of us have formed mental and emotional adhesions that keep us stuck in a narrow range of life experience. We get "comfortable" with behaviors like negative thinking, not taking risks, and thinking we're at the effect of other people and events. As you adopt new parenting behaviors, you may experience discomfort, chaos, or even pain in your change process.

Remember when your first child was born? How many lifestyle and behavior modifications did that life-changing event bring on? One of my friends "forgot," for a moment, that she had a baby one night when she suggested to her husband that they try to catch a movie that was starting in half an hour. I heard of a man who, as was his habit, dumped his clean laundry on the bed to sort it. He just didn't notice his baby happened to be lying there first.

Making a change is like flipping the direction switch on a ceiling fan when it's already moving: it slows down and stops before it reverses its direction. Adopting a new a behavior, like connecting with yourself or breathing before responding to your child, may mean that you're interrupting patterns that have characterized your family (and society) for generations. As you start to make changes, you may even feel some vague sense of disloyalty to your own parents. Or you may feel your own hurt feelings about the way you were parented. Parenting is not for the faint of heart, and an attitude of courage, forgiveness, and acceptance is required to become a parent with soul. Understanding the change process will help you in this adventure.

THE FOUR LEVELS
OF CHANGE

Here's the model William Howell developed. You may have seen it in college or heard it from a motivational speaker. It's become a classic and works well with parenting, learning to ride a bike, or any other behavior or skill you can think of.

THE CHANGE PROCESS			
Level	Your State	Your Experience	What it Takes to Move to the Next Level
Level One	Unconscious Incompetence	You don't know what you don't know.	Knowledge
Level Two	Conscious Incompetence	You know what you don't know.	Notice and Accept Yourself
Level Three	Conscious Competence	You know what you know.	Practice
Level Four	Unconscious Competence	You don't know what you know.	Experiencing the Rewards

LEVEL ONE:
IGNORANCE IS BLISS
...OR IS IT?

Howell coined the term *unconscious incompetence* to describe Level One. At this beginning point, we simply don't know what we don't know. At level one, we may not understand the importance of connecting or the long-term results of neglecting or punishing our child. So, we might read a parenting book or attend a class and learn a more effective way of relating to our child. At that point we have acquired knowledge and move to Level Two.

As you go through your day, you probably see a fair amount of Level One parenting. Remember Trevor and Brittany's mothers at the beginning of this book? This isn't a scientific study, but I'd venture to guess that most of the parenting that goes on in the U.S. that's considered "normal," like yelling, bribing, and threatening is Level One. We as a culture don't know what we don't know about raising kids.

LEVEL TWO:
NO PAIN, NO BLISS

At Level Two we are *consciously incompetent* and now know what we don't know. We realize what we want to change but haven't yet changed it. Yelling at my ten-month-old child and feeling bad about it was Level Two. Though sometimes painful, Level Two marks the beginning of a new direction. Novelist James Baldwin captured the essence of Level Two when he said, "Not everything that is faced can be changed. But nothing can be changed until it is faced." At this stage, some of us may feel embarrassment and regret about how blind we've been. This is a natural step in healing and growth. Level Two is the most painful and frustrating of the four stages. We spend the most time at Level Two, so it's particularly crucial at this stage to be gentle with ourselves. Beating ourselves up and focusing on the negative will keep us stuck in the wasteland of soulless parenting. Only when we accept our imperfection can we move on and become effective.

Noticing is one of the first and most essential steps for changing behavior. We notice something's not working. Perhaps I lose it when our toddler bites the cat. My spouse and I feel so tired we cancel our last two weekly dates. I skip my morning workout three days in a row. Once we've noticed, it's important to love and accept ourselves and our perceived "failures." We must notice and accept to sail smoothly through step two. Many people believe that, in order to change, you must make yourself feel bad and that's simply not true. Stephen Covey, author of *First Things First,* says, "Be patient with yourself. Self-growth is tender; it's holy ground. There's no greater investment." When we love and accept our misbehavior (and our child's), change happens more comfortably, though not always quickly. It feels as if it takes me an average of 287 *noticings* before I change.

Old Self-Talk	New Self-Talk
"I can't believe you did that again."	"I'm learning and part of learning is noticing."

I've seen CEOs of international corporations blanch in dismay when they realize they've mastered the world but seem to have failed as parents. This is precious and sensitive territory for all of us. One of the tools I use for accepting myself is this: when I've "failed," when I've behaved in a way incongruent with my desires or out of alignment with my integrity, I take three deep breaths and say to myself, *Isn't that interesting? I yelled at my child again, forgot to take care of myself this week, and blamed my husband again. Isn't that interesting?* From this place of nonjudgment and discovery, I can calmly choose what I can do next time to improve. *The faster we love and forgive ourselves, the faster we move through Level Two of the change process.*

LEVEL THREE:
THE AWKWARD AWAKENING

When we forgive and accept ourselves, we start to move into Level Three: *Consciously Competent* (knowing what we know). We notice we're using the new behavior and enjoying the rewards, even if we don't do it consistently.

I distinctly remember being at Level Three for a long time when it came to acknowledging feelings. Once I learned (Level Two) how important it was to invite the expression of children's feelings, rather than dismiss them, I committed to this new practice. I started with what I call the Barney Feelings: glad, sad, mad, scared. In the beginning, I stumbled over the new words like someone mangling a new language. "Oh . . . um . . . yes, Brianna, it looks like you're feeling frustrated . . . er . . . mad?"

It's important to understand that, as awkward as we may feel, if our deepest intention is to become the best parents we can be, our kids will pick this up and feel happier. At Level Three we often feel delighted with what we've managed to change. This level requires a great deal of conscious effort or mindfulness. Celebrate each success. Tell yourself exactly what you did and what resulted. Feel the rewards and you will hardwire the new behavior in yourself.

LEVEL FOUR:
SECOND NATURE

At some point we reach Level Four and become *Unconsciously Competent*. Our new behavior is now second nature. The change is so integrated into our being that it's our default mode of operation. Like mastering a bicycle or intercepting the bowl of oatmeal our two-year-old has flipped off the table in her latest physics experiment, we don't have to think.

Level Four feels like parenting bliss, and life hums! No doubt you've already reached Level Four in some areas of parenting. Use your awareness of that success as fuel to encourage you in the areas where there's room for improvement. We achieve Level Four by traversing the previous three levels, and we maintain it by staying connected.

THE UPS AND DOWNS OF CHANGE

Several years ago, a group of my friends and I—all moms—attended a women's ski clinic. We were all good skiers wanting to fine-tune our skills.

The ski instructor watched us ski down a short stretch and then made specific suggestions to each of us. He told me I leaned back a little and that I needed to get my weight forward and centered on my skis. During that two-minute conversation, I moved from Level One (I didn't know I leaned back) to Level Two (I now noticed something that I wanted to change but hadn't yet).

The clinic leader then gave me some suggestions to help me get centered. He instructed me to put my hands far enough in front of me that I could always see them in my peripheral vision. "Easy enough," I quipped, and off I skied. Old habits do die hard. I would start off with my hands in sight (Level Three—I'm Consciously Competent), but after just a few turns my hands would ease back into the old comfort zone (Level Two).

All of us were feeling frustrated, when normally we would be flying down the mountain with ease. We were skiers who rarely fell down, yet that day we were kissing the snow as often as we were enjoying the great views. We used to chat as we skied down the hill, but today everyone was intently focused on building a new skill. Level Three takes a lot of conscious focus. I was skiing down the mountain chanting, "Hands, hands. Where are my hands?" We were all frustrated as we bounced back and forth between Level Two and Level Three. We cursed the ski instructor who had made skiing such a chore! (Much like the woman at the beginning of this chapter cursed me.)

Finally, exasperated, I said, "I can't do this anymore. I have to ski the old way. This is driving me crazy." Ultimately, I decided to work on my new skill only an hour a day, the rest of the day

I would just "be." Over the next few months, I would notice that I was unconsciously centered on the skis. I would touch Level Four. Now after years of practice, it's rare that I get off balance.

Prayer/Affirmation

The Serenity Prayer

God,
Grant me the Serenity
To accept the things I cannot change,
Courage to change the things I can,
And Wisdom to know the difference.

— DR. REINHOLD NIEBUHR,
UNION THEOLOGICAL SEMINARY, 1932

Soulful Reminders

- Parenting with soul is a lifelong practice, not a quick fix, and requires an attitude of courage, forgiveness and acceptance.

- The four levels of change are: unconscious incompetence, conscious incompetence, conscious competence, and unconscious competence.

- As you adopt new parenting behaviors, you may experience discomfort, chaos or even pain in your change process.

THE POWER OF ONE SMALL STEP

Write down one practice you learned or were reminded of in this chapter that you will use this week to remember to be gentle with yourself during the change process. I started by thinking, *isn't that interesting?* Instead of being hard on myself when I made a mistake.

THE CHANGE PROCESS

5

PHILing your child's needs

On the final analysis,
it is your relationship with your child
even more than the use of good techniques
that gets you smoothly through the day.

— LOUISE BATES AMES, PH.D.,
AUTHOR OF *KID COOPERATION:
HOW TO STOP YELLING, NAGGING
AND PLEADING AND GET KIDS TO COOPERATE
AND 30 OTHER BOOKS ON PARENTING*

Now we go for the gold: the connection with your child.

"I don't *know* what was wrong," Kate said tearfully. "My mom was at home everyday. She dressed me in pretty dresses. She put ribbons in my hair and was there everyday after school, but still, *something was missing.*"

Kate was part of an intensive personal growth seminar I led during the nineties. The weekend experience offered a powerful blend of inner child work and group processing, in which the participants had the opportunity to heal the wounds of childhood and choose to create a more positive future. My heart broke to hear the accounts of child abuse so many of the participants had suffered. As sad as these accounts were, another tragic truth emerged over the years. The vast majority of people suffered from a condition more pervasive and insidious than outright abuse. They suffered from what I call Subtle Attachment Disorder (SAD). What Kate and the other course members were missing was *connection.*

Most abuse victims have support groups and names for the various forms of abuse (and therefore a powerful opportunity to heal). SAD victims, however, often go undiagnosed and untreated for a lifetime because this pandemic has not been recognized or named. In fact, it's considered "normal."

As a civilization, we've come a long way. Over the centuries, a "successful" life has progressed from simply surviving to enjoying a certain level of creature comforts. We have the leisure to seek happiness and fulfillment, something few of our great grandparents considered a goal, much less a right. It's no longer legal to sell your child, and children are no longer considered their parents' "property." We love them and want them to live happy, fulfilled lives. We invest our time and money in enriching activities and entertainment, but we often fail to provide what they want and need most to thrive: a strong sense of connection with mom and dad.

Queen Victoria first made it fashionable for parents to separate physically from their children in the 1840s when she popularized the use of the crib and the baby buggy. Until that time, mothers were physically connected to their babies in every culture and still are in many indigenous cultures. We measure our country's progress against headlines like the ones ten years ago when scores of Romanian babies, who had been warehoused and touched very little since birth, were showered with aid from many different nations. These children, who showed retarded physical and emotional growth and stared dull-eyed at their rescuers, were diagnosed as having Reactive Attachment Disorder, or RAD (an "official" diagnosis). This disorder is not limited to children in orphanages. Children develop RAD as a result of failing to bond with their caregiver in their formative early years and the reasons can be myriad: physical abandonment, mother's illness, child's illness, caregiver's inability to connect, and more. More recently, we've witnessed the extreme effects of failing to connect on an everyday basis in the form of murder and violence in our schools.

I feel deeply concerned about the long-term effects of both RAD and SAD on our culture and on the world. Households are filled with people who don't know each other. As parents, we may love our children, make sure they eat healthy, enroll them in the finest schools, and yet, never know their souls. Husbands don't know their wives, parents don't know their teens, and grandparents don't know their grandchildren.

MASTERING THE MAIN INGREDIENT

How often do you ask yourself, "What is my child's state of being?" Not the state of the house or the toys, but your child's internal emotional environment. Study after study has concluded that a feeling of "connectedness" is the *single most important factor* in a child's success and happiness. According to Robert W. Blum, M.D., coauthor of an enormous research project that examined high-risk behaviors by teens, "The most effective way to protect young people from unhealthy or dangerous behaviors is for parents to be involved in their lives." *Connected to their own lives and to their children's lives.*

We don't have to become dictators or self-sacrificing saints. We don't necessarily need to march the kids off to a therapist. We just have to *connect*. Name one other practice that:

- **Dramatically increases your child's level of cooperation**

- **Helps decrease misbehavior**

- **Motivates your child to listen better**

- **Creates more harmony in your home**

- **Brings you profound peace of mind**

Our connection to our children colors our parenting experience more than anything else. So, it's essential that we make it our number one priority. If you take the time to connect, the grocery shopping will go more easily, the power struggles will decrease, communication lines will open, and you'll feel better about how you parent.

Imagine someone you feel connected to, like a close friend. If she asked you for a favor, wouldn't you go out of your way to help? If someone you don't feel connected with (like the relative or coworker who only calls when he needs something) asks a favor, wouldn't you be less inclined to offer support? Children feel the same way. When they're experiencing a strong connection with us, they naturally want to maintain that connection and harmony by listening and cooperating. I'm not suggesting you raise your child to be a "people-pleaser" or someone who's blindly obedient and motivated by fear. Instead, I want you to experience the feeling of harmony and ease that emerges when we feel lovingly linked to another.

PHIL 'EM UP

Establishing this connection starts when we become aware of children's four emotional needs and the importance of meeting them. The acronym for the four needs is *PHIL*: Children need to feel *Powerful, Heard, Important,* and *Loved*. In their every interaction with the world around them and us, children come to conclusions about themselves: *I am loved. I am a burden. I am wanted. I was an accident. I am important. I am not important.* Understand this truth and you take a big step toward creating a strong connection with your child.

Children, like adults, want to feel the authentic *Power* that comes from having influence and input about their environment. They want to be *Heard* and understood, not just the words they say, but the essence of their communications. They long to be heard in an accepting, nonjudgmental atmosphere. They want to feel *Important,* that what they have to say matters and that they're valuable enough to warrant their parents' love and attention. They also need to feel unconditionally *Loved*. Loved for who they are, not what they do. Loved simply because they exist. True connection fills all four of these needs.

And most parents don't realize this.

Children Need to Feel *PHIL*ed:

Powerful

Heard

Important

Loved

LET ME EXPERIENCE MY POWER

Children thrive when they feel that they have influence over their life experience. Just like adults, they long to have choices and control. When parents can meet this natural need to feel powerful, they'll raise confident, connected children.

To successfully meet this need, we must let go of our desire to control and begin to see life through our children's eyes. If you find yourself getting into frequent power struggles, ask yourself a new question. When faced with a defiant child, the most common self-talk I hear from parents is *How can I get my child to do what I want?* When we change the question to *How can I help my child feel powerful in this situation without compromising myself?* We open the door to a whole new paradigm in parenting.

I'm not suggesting you let your child rule the home or that you cater to your child's every whim. Ironically, spoiling your child (the behavior at the opposite end of the power continuum from controlling) is just as damaging to a child's self-confidence, if not more so. Many child psychologists report that their most difficult clients come from homes that are too permissive. When parents do not set limits, children often decide their parents don't care. When parents lovingly set limits and offer opportunities for children to experience authentic power, connection happens.

When my older daughter Brianna was three and a half years old, she decided she was through with car seats. Every time we got into the car, she loudly refused to get into the car seat. I felt exasperated, especially since I had a six-month-old baby to buckle in as well. On a few stressful occasions on days when I probably hadn't taken care of myself, I ended the power struggle by forcing her into the car seat. She screamed the whole way home. Afterward, I felt terrible!

Then, one day, I remembered the four needs and the question I needed to ask myself to diffuse the struggle: *How can I give my child more power in this situation?*

I came up with a plan. At that time, Brianna loved pretending to be the "Queen of Everything." One day, I sat down with her and said, "I know you like to be the Queen. Would you like to be the Queen of the car?"

"Yes!" she replied exuberantly.

"All right, then here are your duties as Queen: Once we get in the car, you need to make sure that everyone is buckled in their seat belt or car seat before the car can move. Only after you tell me that everyone is buckled in, will I start driving."

I didn't know if it would work, but I knew I had sincerely searched for a way to give her more influence over her situation. It worked! Brianna delighted in her new job as the "Queen of the Car." Her reign lasted for months. Then one day, I got out of the car to get the mail and when I got back in to drive down our drive-way to the garage, I heard, "No, no, no. We can't go. You're not buckled!" This was a critical point, because if I refused to buckle up to drive down our driveway, then her power was not authentic. So for the next few months, I buckled up to drive the 50 feet to the garage.

PLEASE HEAR ME

While waiting several hours in an airport on our way back from a family vacation, our daughters, who were seven and ten, befriended two sisters about the same age. In a short time, the four girls firmly bonded. After hearing the boarding announcement, my six-year-old ran over to me and excitedly announced, "We're in row six and they're in row seven!" She was delirious with joy. "That *is* exciting," I said. As she ran back to join the group of girls, I noticed her new friend approaching her father to share the same news. "Dad, we're in row seven and they're in row six!"

He didn't so much as glance up from the book he was reading. No half-hearted nod. Nothing. Just a scowl.

"Daddy, isn't that exciting?"

Still no response. His eyes never left the page. She tried a few more times to engage him, but to no avail. I watched her enthusiasm spiral down into disappointment as she shrugged and ran back to join the game of tag the other girls had started.

I heaved a big sigh. Ouch! The sting of the interaction had touched a chord deep within me. In an instant I was taken back to the pain of being a child in similar situations and deciding over and over I was utterly unimportant. I also felt sad because this dad had reflected back to me a part of myself I did not like—a disconnected way of being with children that permeates our society.

HELP ME FEEL IMPORTANT

Children spell love T-I-M-E. Each moment of fully connected time you spend with them is a deposit in their reservoir of self-love and self-esteem. The word important means *marked by or indicative of significant worth or consequence: valuable in content or relationship.* Each time you ask their opinion or pay attention in some other connected way, they value themselves more. A parent's freely given attention conveys a simple but significant message: "You are important to me." Author Yehuda Berg, a leading authority on Kabbalah, captured the essence of this truth, saying, "Kabbalah taught me that when I play with my children, I must truly enter into their world, not just put in time with them." For our child to experience the finest sort of parenting, our intention must be to "enter into their world" and make connection a way of life.

LET ME KNOW I'M LOVED

It was a *dark day* at the Falcone home. It's always a dark day when mommy is unhappy.

I had yelled at my children all morning. I was not being nice!

I barked, "Put your breakfast dishes into the dishwasher. Pick up the toys. Wash your hands. No snacks before lunch. Be nice to your sister!" I wasn't exactly walking the Parenting with Soul talk that day.

The final straw came as I tripped on the stairs over the markers I had asked the kids to pick up all morning. *I lost it.* "Get down here *right now* and pick up this stuff before somebody gets killed on these stairs!" I screeched.How did my eight-year-old respond in the face of such unrelenting verbal abuse?

"Mommy, it looks like you need a hug."

I felt overwhelmed with intense emotions, astonished at her serenity, her perception, and her ability to detach! I felt horrible.

Mostly, I felt overcome with the unconditional love that oozed from heras she approached me with outstretched arms. How could she love and accept me in this, one of my darkest hours? What kind of child could love and accept and hug her parent when all she had received that morning was my negativity?

The rest of the day, I asked myself *What did I do that contributed to my child's loving response this morning?* I had an inkling. It probably had to do with giving her that kind of unconditional love and acceptance thousands of times.

Children live what they are taught.

PRACTICE *PHIL* AND SPOIL THE CHILD?

We'd been discussing the steps for connecting in a parenting class, when Alisha, the mother of a three-year-old boy named Jessie, voiced a concern during the break: "If I give Jessie all this attention, won't he just want more and more and more?"

Actually the opposite happens. A medical study in the early nineties demonstrated this principle in a powerful way. Doctors noticed that many post-surgical patients felt frustrated calling a nurse, asking for pain medication, then waiting 20 minutes to an hour for the overloaded nurse to get the medication and give it to them.

A program called PCA (Patient Controlled Anesthesia) enabled post-surgical patients to push a button whenever they needed pain medication and inject a small amount directly into their bloodstream. If that little bit weren't enough, they could push again and get a little more and continue until their pain was under control, up to a specified limit. At first, many doctors and nurses worried that people would take much more of the pain medication than they needed. However, the exact opposite occurred. Since patients knew they were in control and could get the pain medicine at any time, they actually used much less medication—sometimes as much as 50 percent less!

In a similar way, connecting with your child does not create the "bottomless" well of need that many parents fear. Instead, it often decreases clingy and needy behavior once the balance of connection is restored. However, if your child has been deprived of your attention, he may act very needy until he feels convinced that a connection with you is readily available. If you do feel you have shortchanged your children, the best you can do is honestly and lovingly assess your connection practice (Level Two of the change process: notice and accept) and make the changes needed to reconnect. Hang in there. It will happen.

PHIL ALERTS

Misbehavior happens when children inappropriately seek to fill the hunger for the four core needs. Power struggles erupt when children feel powerless. Children *scream* for attention when they don't feel heard or important. Lee London, a fellow parenting instructor who works with inner-city gangs in Detroit, points out that gangs do meet these four core needs. But so does giving children the power and control at appropriate times, really hearing them, and making time for them. Psychologist and philosopher William James said, "The deepest principle in human nature is the craving to be appreciated."

When your children decide you are not available to meet their needs, the progression looks like this: First, they get louder in an attempt to get your attention. If they are not feeling *Powerful, Heard, Important,* or *Loved,* they feel discouraged. If they still have not captured your attention, they usually get quiet and give up. They quit making requests because they learn that the connection is not available.

PHIL Alerts

First children get louder.
Then they get discouraged.
Then they get quiet.
Then they give up.

Stop right now and ask yourself the following four questions:

- **What is one step I can take to help my child feel more powerful?**

- **What is one step I can take to help my child feel heard?**

- **What is one step I can take to help my child feel important?**

- **What is one step I can take to help my child feel loved?**

In your next interaction with your child, instead of asking yourself *How can I get my child to* _____? change the question to *What is my child trying to tell me?* Jump at the chance to discover your child's need then help—*PHIL* it.

When your child knows a fulfilling connection with you is readily available, it's like an ongoing intravenous self-esteem drip or a high-speed Internet line to your heart that's always live. They know they can easily tap into the power of your love and get what they want at any time. They feel better about themselves. They naturally feel less needy, so they behave in a way that's less demanding. They feel *PHILed*—powerful, heard, important, and loved. In fact, they feel *adored*.

PHIL IS GOOD
FOR YOUR HEALTH

By now you may be convinced of the power of *PHIL* to enhance your children's emotional health, and several studies correlate family closeness to physical health as well. In a follow-up to the Harvard Mastery of Stress Study, Gary Schwartz, Ph.D., and Linda Russek, Ph.D. of the University of Arizona, looked at how college students who had reported having loving parents fared 35 years later, when in their 50s. They found that having been loved as a child correlated to good health later in life. Among the men who had, decades earlier, rated their parents as not very loving, 87 percent had a chronic physical illness compared to 25 percent of the men who had rated their parents as loving.

In another study, researchers tracking 1,100 medical students at Johns Hopkins University in the 1940s found that men who developed cancer had more frequently described a lack of closeness to their parents 50 years earlier, compared to men who were cancer-free. In fact, according to a 1982 report in the *Journal of Behavioral Medicine*, the best predictor of who would get cancer later in life was not smoking or drinking, but the closeness of father-son relationships!

All in all, *PHIL* is one of our most powerful practices for body, mind, and spirit. "Satisfying human relationships can be the most healing 'medication' of all," says Chloe Madanes, L.H.D., director of the Family Therapy Institute of Washington. "No amount of exercise, meditation, massage, stress reduction, or broccoli is an adequate substitute for love and affection for promoting health."

THE MOST IMPORTANT RULE
IN THE WORLD

Philosophers have been speculating on the rules of human relationships for thousands of years, and out of all that speculation, there has evolved only one important precept. It is not new. It is as old as history. Zoroaster taught it to his followers in Persia 2500 years ago. Confucius preached it in China 24 centuries ago. Lao-Tse, the founder of Taoism, taught it to his disciples in the Valley of the Han. Buddha preached it on the bank of the Holy Ganges 500 years before Christ. The sacred books of Hinduism taught it 1,000 years before that. Jesus taught it among the stony hills of Judea 19 centuries ago. Jesus summed it up in one thought—probably the most important rule in the world: "Do unto others as you would have others do unto you."

— DALE CARNEGIE,
HOW TO WIN FRIENDS AND INFLUENCE PEOPLE

Prayer/Affirmation

When I help my child feel PHILed,
I fulPHIL my divine mission as a parent.

Soulful Reminders

- Study after study has concluded that a feeling of "connectedness" is the single most import factor in a child's success and happiness.

- The vast majority of people suffer from Subtle Attachment Disorder (SAD) that results from a lack of genuine connection with their parents.

- Children need to feel
  - ➡ Powerful
  - ➡ Heard
  - ➡ Important
  - ➡ Loved

- When your children decide you are not available to meet their needs, they get louder in an attempt to get your attention, they feel discouraged, they get quiet, and then they give up.

- **Several long-term studies correlate family closeness with physical health.**

- **When children know they can easily tap into the power of your love and get what they want at any time, they feel better about themselves.**

THE POWER OF
ONE SMALL STEP

Write down one practice you learned or were reminded of in this chapter that you will use this week to help your child feel *Powerful, Heard, Important,* and *Loved.* I started by getting in the habit of asking myself, "What is my child trying to communicate to me—which need are they asking me to *PHIL?*"

6

move toward your child with love: how to connect with your child

There are two types of people—
those who come into a room and say,
"Well, here I am,"
and those who come in and say,
"Ah, there you are."

— FREDERICK COLLINS

The next level of connecting with your child is especially effective and important in challenging and very ordinary situations.

One evening my younger daughter Alexa felt so excited at having company, she couldn't sit still. "Do you want to see my new toy? Let me show you this refrigerator magnet. Can I give you a neck massage?" She was wired for sound and must have gotten up from the dinner table nine or ten times within the first five minutes.

The way I handled this situation made me feel proud of how far I'd come. The old way would have been to order her back to the table and if she didn't listen, I would speak louder or give a warning. Since I had learned about *PHIL,* I was now committed to finding a more peaceful way to get her to remain seated and eat dinner with us. I stood up, walked over to where she was demonstrating a new dance she'd learned, bent over so my face was near hers, smiled, made friendly eye contact, and said, "Alexa, do you know why I'm here?"

Her face lit up and she burst out laughing. "You want me to sit down!" she replied with glee and laughed all the way back to the table, where she remained seated for the rest of dinner.

CONNECTION 101

The single most powerful connecting practice is to move toward your child with love. This one skill has transformed my family life more than anything else. With practice, this will become second nature and the rewards will be well worth the time you invest to learn this move.

I think the reason this connecting approach works is that we're not only reminding our child of our unconditional love as we draw near them and look deeply into their soul, but we're connecting on an essence level. Our child's inner essence feels deeply touched by ours. And when that happens, peace and harmony are instantaneous, even if we are disciplining them.

You may find it handy to have some step-by-step instructions if you, like many of us, did not experience great modeling of this skill in childhood and, therefore, are not already Masters of Connection. Here are the steps I find most helpful:

How to Move Toward Your Child with Love

- **Set your intention to connect**
- **Smile**
- **Get down on their level**
- **Give friendly eye contact**
- **Lovingly touch your child**
- **Give all your focused attention**
- **Use few words**
- **Give information or ask a question**

Step One: Set your intention to connect. Before you approach your children, whether they are playing quietly or embroiled in a fight, take a moment to affirm your desire to use this moment to connect. It's easy to get in the habit of approaching our children with disconnecting thoughts *(This child demands so much attention),* commands *(He'd better get in that tub without a fight tonight),* or judgments *(I'm so sick of you two arguing).* It takes a strong conscious effort to overcome negative thought patterns. The habit of taking three deep breaths will help you remember to set your intention to connect with your child.

Step Two: Smile. A smile instantly relaxes the muscles and eases tension in your face. Thich Nhat Hanh says, "A tiny bud of a smile on our lips nourishes awareness and calms us miraculously. It returns us to the peace we thought we had lost." We don't always feel like smiling, especially when our child is doing something we strongly want them to stop. I suggest you "fake it 'til you make it" and "act as if." Psychologist and philosopher, William James, was talking about these two practices when he said, "Action seems to follow feeling, but really action and feeling go together; and by regulating the action, which is under the more direct control of the will, we can indirectly regulate the feeling which is not. Thus, the sovereign voluntary path to cheerfulness, if our cheerfulness be lost, is to sit up cheerfully and to act and speak as if cheerfulness were already there . . ."

Intention is the key. That way you won't be wearing a forced smile that says, *you'd better do this,* which will feel like manipulation to a child—and backfire. The simple act of wearing a slight smile does wonders. Think Mona Lisa here, not high school cheerleader, and remember the words of Mother Teresa, "You can give the poor even your life, but if you don't do it with a smile, you give them nothing."

Step Three: Get down on their level. That might mean sitting on the floor or squatting. Or, bring them up to your level. Either way, you establish rapport. I used to teach this same practice in customer service seminars. Getting on someone else's level balances the power in a tangible way and demonstrates your intention to come closer to them. It says *You are important and I want to hear you*—helping your child to feel *PHIL*ed.

Step Four: Give friendly eye contact. Smile with your eyes. Look into the child's left eye, which is connected with the right, or feeling side, of his brain. This isn't a flicker, a glimpse, or a glance. Smile for three beats or for one deep breath. *Connect with your child's soul.*

Step Five: Lovingly touch your child. My family was eating breakfast in a restaurant in Cabo San Lucas, Mexico. A mother and her 13-year-old son were seated next to us. Throughout the meal, the mother lovingly touched her son, caressing his arm and hair. They were very physically affectionate and I commented to my husband how rare it would be to observe such a scene in the States.

Using loving touch, we can capture our child's attention and show our love at the same time. Loving touch is healing, essential to our emotional well-being, and unfortunately, a rare commodity in many homes. If you have older children and are not in the habit of touching them, start slowly, remembering that your intention is nearly as important as your touch. You may want to silently say *I love and care about you* before you reach out. If you are a parent of very young children, begin touching early on.

Step Six: Give all your focused attention. Put down your cup of coffee. Stop eating. Set the newspaper aside. Let go of the world situation, what you want from your child, or what you're going to do or say next and give 100 percent of your attention to your child. Breathing is permissible and strongly encouraged!

Step Seven: Use few words. Listen 80 percent of the time and talk only 20 percent. Perhaps all you say is, "Hi!" Respond with genuine interest to whatever your child says. Often our first response to a parenting challenge is to spew. There is no such thing as a basic human need to be spewed upon. Yet spew we do, especially if we're parents. When we offer comments, suggestions, and lectures without first hearing the child, we disconnect. If we continually respond this way, over time our children develop a condition called "mommy deafness."

This step reminds me of the verse, "Let thy speech be short, comprehending much in few words." (Eccl 32:8) Notice how few of the points above involve talking. A big part of Parenting with Soul is like the soul—invisible. We often fool ourselves when we talk. "The biggest problem of communication is the illusion that it has been achieved," according to one anonymous master. Words rarely teach. How strange we offer so many.

Step Eight: Give information or ask a question. When you speak, start by giving information, not giving commands or interrogating. I recently saw a great example of the power of asking a question instead of giving a command on a bumper sticker on an 18-wheeler. It read, "If I stop, can you?" The question got me thinking: "Could I stop in time?" When we question instead of command, children respond by thinking instead of reacting. This last point reminds me of a book title Brianna came up with one day after I'd forgotten to follow my own advice: *Ways to Tell Your Kids Things without Yelling.*

These eight moves are a way to communicate with your child without yelling, nagging, pleading, threatening, manipulating, or worse. When we use negative motivators, we risk damaging our relationship with our child—the most valuable parenting asset we possess.

One day a student in my parenting class, who had not yet learned the "move toward you child with love" approach, offered a familiar lament: "I yell because it gets results. I feel so bad about myself that I can't take it anymore. My son wants nothing to do with me. I'm a bad mother." Like so many of us, she had been raised with negative motivators and used these with her five-year-old. As a result, their relationship was strained, which lessened her chances of getting cooperation. Several weeks after learning and practicing these eight moves, she tearfully reported, "My son is actually happy to see me again."

WHEN TO MOVE TOWARD YOUR CHILD WITH LOVE

Nearly any time is a good time to move toward your child with love. Here are some specific ideas:

When They Feel Content: We naturally tend to pay attention to our child when he is misbehaving. If, however, you pass by the family room and notice he's engrossed with his Tonka Trucks, you may think *Now's my chance! I'll run and put the lasagna in the oven.* Instead, get into the habit of spontaneously moving toward your child. *Make it a habit to spontaneously move toward your children with love several times each day.* Move toward your child with love when they are content once a day for seven days and watch what happens.

To Calm a Fight: In the Redirecting Children's Behavior course, Kathryn Kvols says, "Bring peace to the fight." When we feel frustrated or angry as we approach our fighting children, we add those energies to the fight. What we really want is to facilitate a peaceful (and instant) resolution. If we stop for just a moment to breathe (I usually have time for only one breath) and set our intention to bring a bit more peace as we approach the fight, magic happens.

Magic? This woman does not know my children. I can almost hear your resistance because when I introduce this in the parenting class, parents furiously challenge me. I explain to them that this works because children, just like everyone else, naturally gravitate toward the energy that surrounds them. Therefore, we do have the power to influence the direction of the energy in any situation. You've most likely witnessed this. When you walk into a room feeling happy, you are more likely to elicit smiles than if you storm in upset.

The first time I brought peace to a fight, I stunned my children into silence. "What are you doing?" asked my four-year-old. The new way was radically different from previous interventions. Even the skeptics in my class who try this report back with similar results.

Here is some helpful self-talk to try on the way to the fight:

Old Self-Talk	New Self-Talk
"I am so sick and tired of these kids fighting!"	"I can set my intention to bring peace to the fight."

When You or They are Making a Request: One of the first times I got to use the eight steps for connecting was with a child I did not know well. We attended an outdoor concert with several families, including one we'd recently met. Early in the day, I found myself annoyed with their eight-year-old son. He had a pattern of interrupting his mother by first calling, "Mommy," in the middle of her conversations. She usually ignored him, to which he replied even louder, *"Moooooooom."* Then he would burst into the last phase of his three-step assault, a loud chant, *"Mom!"* *"Mom!"* *"Mom!"* *"Mom!"* until the exasperated mom would snap, "What do you want?" All the adults were going nuts.

This boy just wants to be heard, I thought to myself. *Can I find a way to respectfully set a limit with him?* I devised a two-step plan. First, if he tried to get my attention, I decided to respond to him as quickly as possible so he would feel heard by me. Soon after I had set my intention, he interrupted his mother with his *ascending three-step maneuver* while I was talking to her. I turned to him, lovingly touched him, smiled and looked into his eyes. He was taken aback and instantly got quiet. "William," I asked, "will you do me a favor?" "What?" he asked. "When your mom and I are talking and you need to ask her something, could you place your hand on me? When you do that, I'll stop as soon as I finish my sentence." "Uh, okay," he stammered.

A few hours later, I was talking with his mother and he approached. Though he didn't place his hand on me, he deliberately used a very soft voice and as I had promised, I allowed him to ask his mother the question. I then thanked him for using a soft voice.

After a Separation: When we arrive to pick our children up from daycare, a play date, or birthday party, they are sometimes reluctant to leave. Instead of repeating, "Come on, let's go," move toward your child and use the eight connecting steps to get their attention. You can expect more cooperation and a smoother exit.

My friend Paul went to Amman, Jordan, while he was in the Army to practice emergency medicine and noticed immediately that their culture has a much greater focus on relationships than the United States does. Jordanians make a big deal about saying hello. Paul particularly enjoyed the custom of standing whenever anyone entered or left a room. He said he felt so acknowledged and warmly greeted, even if no words were exchanged. Upon returning to the states, he missed that warm feeling of connection, so he's made a ritual of greeting people, saying hello, and standing up to introduce them. When his wife comes home, no matter how he feels, he stops what he's doing and makes a little special occasion about the fact that she is home. And she does the same for him. Become a conscious greeter whenever your child returns home or enters a room. *Ah, there you are* is a noble aim for all of our connecting experiences.

If you're a parent who works outside the home, you may find T. Berry Brazelton's advice particularly helpful:

> "Learn to save up energy in the workplace for homecoming. Plan for children to fall apart when you arrive home after work. They've saved up their strongest feelings all day." He suggests that when you get home you gather your children together and "sit in a big rocking chair until everyone is close again. When children squirm to get down, you can turn to chores and housework."

When You Want to Get Their Attention: My daughters invited their five-year-old friend over to spend the afternoon, and they were all seated at the kitchen table waiting for dinner.

I asked, "Who wants broccoli with their mac and cheese?"

No response. They weren't necessarily talking loudly, they were just engrossed in their conversation.

"Who would like broccoli?" Again, no reply. I was standing only three feet from them. I asked a third time and got the same. I decided to connect. I moved toward our guest with my friendly face and calmly placed a hand on her shoulder. She was surprised and amused and started laughing. I didn't even have to say anything. All three children then gave me their answer.

Increasing the decibel level when we're not feeling heard is the shortest route, but often disconnects us from our children. This way of reaching your child takes more effort in the beginning, but

I think you will find, as I did, that the increased joy and harmony you experience will more than motivate you to take the time to connect.

Instead of Yelling or Threatening: One night after a parenting class, a father of two boys ages three and five approached me and said, "Vickie, this stuff might work on girls, but not on boys. You don't have boys, so you don't understand. I have to *get in their face* to get their attention."

"What is your tone of voice when you get in their face?" I asked.

The dad laughed. "I've had it, usually, and I'm mad."

I empathized with him. I've been there at the end of the proverbial rope, resorting to the quickest technique I know—yelling. "Continue to get in their face," I insisted. "Just do it with love. Instead of getting 'loud and nasty,' try 'close and kind.' Both get the results you want, and the latter doesn't hurt the child."

It's true that we get better results when we *get in their face*. This father had been practicing a truncated version of the eight steps. He made eye contact, used not-so-loving touch and gave the boys 100 percent of his focused attention. He just needed to add a few more steps to increase his likelihood for cooperation while, at the same time, preserving his relationship with his sons. At the next class, the father shared that, though he had not mastered all the steps, even adding a few made his interactions with his sons go more smoothly.

As a Regular Family Activity: One way to make a commitment to the practice of moving toward your child with love is to put it on the calendar. I've known families in which each child got a special time alone with each parent once a week or once a month, and the children eagerly looked forward to it. In another family, the grandparents had a tradition of taking each grandchild on a trip to Disneyland when they turned eight.

My friend moved to Salt Lake City when she was in junior high and immediately noticed bumper stickers all over town that said, "You won't be reading this on a Monday night." The Mormons have a practice called Family Home Evening, which we all might want to adopt and adapt: Once a week, usually on Monday nights, families gather for family-centered spiritual training and social activities. What form might this take in your home?

MOVE TOWARD EVERYONE WITH LOVE

Moving toward someone with love will help you make a meaningful connection with your significant other, friends, and at work as well—especially when it's the last thing you may want to do. One day at the gym I was working out on a machine in front of the TV and an acquaintance named Steven asked if I would mind if he turned on the TV. I overcame my people-pleasing programming and answered, "Yes." "Why?" he asked. I said, "I really don't like TV." His disappointment was noticeable, especially when his friend walked up and said, "Hey Steven, turn on the TV." "We can't," he said. "She was here first and doesn't want it on."

He and his friend got on machines a few down from mine. The air turned icy. I was glad I'd had the courage to ask for what I wanted, but felt real strain between us. When I finished my workout, about ten minutes later, I wanted to just walk to the dressing room and be done with the tension. Instead, I mustered the courage to walk over to Steven, smile, make eye contact, and say, "Thank you for humoring me." He exhaled and connected with me and the good feelings between us were rekindled. It was not so much my words that healed the strain as my intention to connect.

WHAT MY INTERNET PROVIDER TAUGHT ME ABOUT CONNECTING

My Internet provider raised my consciousness about connecting with my children. One day as I logged off one online service and onto another, a message box appeared on my screen. The title of the box was "Auto Disconnect" and the message read: "Do you want to close this connection?" I had to click on "Disconnect Now," or "Stay Connected."

AUTO DISCONNECT

Do you want to close this connection?

Click one:

DISCONNECT NOW   STAY CONNECTED

It was a message I had read hundreds of times, but on this day it held new meaning. I realized that for me this message box symbolized the moment-to-moment decisions I make while interacting with my children.

"Disconnect Now" or "Stay Connected?" It's a choice we face hundreds of times each day. And the sum total of these choices shape our parenting experience *and* our child's self esteem. Get into the habit of asking yourself, "Does this activity connect me or disconnect me from my child?" If the answer is "disconnect," choose a connecting practice instead.

IT'S NOT WHAT YOU DO; IT'S THE WAY THAT YOU DO IT

One evening a woman came up to me just before my class began and said, "You know that hand thingy? I used it and it didn't work." She was referring to Step Five: Lovingly touch your child. It doesn't work when we use it like a technique. She didn't have the thought *How can I connect with my child?* It was more like *If I use this, I can get my child to do what I want.* Your intention is crucial. You don't need parenting tools and techniques when you truly connect with your child.

A coaching client called me one day to ask more about connecting.

"What activities would you suggest I do with my children to connect more with them?"

"It's not about the *activity*," I told her. "It's *never* about the activity. It's about the quality of the connection, whether you are engaged in an activity or not."

"What do you mean?" she asked. I then described how to move toward your child with love.

"Then, how do *you* connect with your children?" she asked. "For example, what did you do last week? Give me some ideas!" My mind went blank; I could not think of any specific things I had done to connect with my children during the past week. I did agree to write down all the connecting moments I could in the upcoming week and report back to her in seven days. Here's my list:

- When my seven-year-old was quietly playing solitaire on the computer, I sat down in the chair with her, became interested in the game, and played with her. (Moved toward my child with love while she was content)

- I invited the girls to help me cut up vegetables to feed the hamster. (Set my intention to connect)

- When my ten-year-old said, "Come with me to do my homework," I let go of a cleaning project, went into her room, and sat on her bed for about half an hour while she did her homework. We had intermittent conversations about her new erasers, an upcoming birthday party, and how much she liked her teacher. (Moved toward my child while she was content)

- When they arrived home from school, I sat down, made eye contact, and listened to the details of their day, consciously choosing to talk very little. It was amazing how much they had to say when I made the "space." (Used few words)

- When the girls got home from school, I got off the phone and asked if they wanted to go next door to our rental apartment to see the new carpet that had been installed that day. I then watched them dance around and run through the apartment. When I was ready to leave and they were not, I gave them a few more minutes since I was not rushed. (Set my intention to connect, smiled, gave all of my focused attention, offered friendly eye contact)

- We went to get ice cream; I made friendly eye contact, and really enjoyed the ice cream and company of my family. (Offered friendly eye contact and used few words)

- On the way home from the grocery store, the girls asked to stop in a second-hand store. Again, since I was not on a time schedule (and, yes, often I am!) I patiently watched them try on and model high-heeled shoes. (Gave all of my focused attention)

Not too glamorous is it? Can you see that it's about *being*, rather than *doing*? You do not have to add any special activities, just be fully present using the eight steps to move toward your child with love.

To look at this from another angle, consider the activities we typically think of as connecting, "quality family time" that can turn out to be just the opposite, depending on our ability and desire to connect:

Family Vacations: Fun in the sun, creating lasting memories, connecting with the family: the things that family vacations are made of, right? Not always. Just because we're two thousand miles from home in a tropical paradise doesn't insure a connecting experience. I witnessed this first hand at the front desk of our property management company in Aspen for years. "How can these people be so miserable in Aspen?" we'd ask. The answer of course was because they were also miserable in Hollywood, New York, or Miami. I observed the same disconnected behavior in many of the theme parks we visited while in San Diego a few years ago. Moms and dads on cell phones, yelling, threatening, and spanking their children, babies overtired to the point of exhaustion.

A man at Legoland took the cake. We were waiting in the line for the parachute ride and he was talking nonstop on his cell phone. A few minutes later I looked up to see him on the ride with his young son, still talking on his cell phone! He talked all the way through the ride.

Dining Out: I heard about an international example of the SAD epidemic in Breckenridge, a Colorado ski resort. A mother, father, and four-year-old boy from Italy walked in to the most popular breakfast spot. Both parents were engaged in animated conversations on their cell phones. As soon as they were seated, the child took out a hand-held computer game and began playing it. They only spoke when the waitress came for their order.

I've seen countless acts of child abuse in restaurants all over the country that have ranged from name calling to humiliating and spanking. We spend money on expensive outings and nice restaurants, but remember that, better a dry crust with peace and quiet than a house full of feasting, with strife.

Family Meetings: One of the most connecting parts at the Falcone household is the family meeting on Monday nights. For the most part, our family meetings are fun and uplifting. It is a time for everyone to be heard and encouraged and to plan some fun activities together. I will admit that, even though my intention is to connect, sometimes the meetings spiral down into arguments about chores and dirty socks. We've had tears at more than one meeting.

A friend of mine from high school shared a tale of a far more disconnected kind of family meeting. She said that no one was ever happy at her family meetings. Her father used the meetings as a time to scold, punish, and complain. This was a big disconnection. On one occasion, he took the meeting to an all-time low. She had been struggling with anorexia and was in and out of treatment programs. At one of the family meetings, he turned to her in front of the family and snapped, "Do you know how much you have cost me with this eating disorder thing?" *Ouch!*

IF YOU WANT SOME RESPECT, YOU'VE GOT TO CONNECT

All of these principles work with preteens, even if their signals differ. Michelle, a single mother of two boys ages nine and eleven, felt despondent over the almost nonexistent communication and connection with her sons. She claimed that the only communication in their home was related to logistics. "Did you do your homework? Where's your backpack? Dinner's ready." The boys, especially the older one, answered most questions with a single word. One night in the Parenting with Soul class, the group brainstormed some ideas for how she could connect with her older son. She went home with one practice, which she tried the next night. After finishing his homework, her older son usually retreated to his room to listen to music. She decided she would stop cleaning the kitchen and join him instead. The next week she reported her experience to the class. "I went into his room and just sat on the bed. He didn't quite know what to do at first, but I asked a few questions about his music and he started talking."

"What happened next?" I asked.

Choked with tears now, she said, "Every time I got up to leave the room, he said, 'Don't go yet.' So I stayed in his room until 10:45 on a school night."

Often, all we have to do is move toward our children with an open attitude, a desire to connect, and no agenda. As often as possible throughout the day, stop what you're doing and follow your child's lead. If she's got something special to share with you, or he's fussing for no specific reason, drop everything and connect. That's when miracles happen.

Prayer/Affirmation

I consciously embrace
the opportunities in my day
to move toward my child with love.
As I do, I lovingly lay the foundation for a relationship
with my child that is close and mutually respectful.

Soulful Reminders

- The single most powerful connecting practice is to move toward your child with love.

- To connect with your child:
    - ➠ Set your intention to connect
    - ➠ Smile
    - ➠ Get down on their level
    - ➠ Give friendly eye contact
    - ➠ Give all your focused attention
    - ➠ Use few words
    - ➠ Take a breath before replying
    - ➠ Give information or ask a question

- Move toward your child with love:
    - ➠ When they are content
    - ➠ To calm a fight
    - ➠ When you, or they, are making a request
    - ➠ After a separation
    - ➠ When you want to get their attention
    - ➠ Instead of yelling or threatening
    - ➠ As a regular family activity

- Connecting is never about the activity. It's about the quality of the connection, whether or not you are engaged in an activity.

- You can also move toward older children and other adults with love.

THE POWER OF
ONE SMALL STEP

Write down one practice you learned or were reminded of in this chapter that you will use this week to move toward your child with love. I started by setting my intention to connect before approaching my children.

7

the four moves to a connected life

To make connection a habit, a lifestyle, and an environment in which your child will blossom and grow, commit to these four moves:

- **Recognize the call to connect**

- **Practice high level connecting everyday**

- **Invite your child to "come here," not, "go there"**

- **Put connection before logistics**

Let's look at each of these elements in a bit more detail.

THE FIRST MOVE: RECOGNIZE THE CALL TO CONNECT

Disconnection is what happens when we don't recognize the call to connect. Recently my friend Lori asked me for advice about bedtime power struggles with her three-year-old. She said that when she put her daughter Katelyn to bed each night, she would come out of her room again and again and again. "Mom, I need a drink of water . . . I'm scared in my room . . . I want to sleep with my brother." In addition, Katelyn was waking up in the middle of the night and going into her parent's bedroom. One night, Lori felt so frustrated (after the tenth trip out of the room) that she spanked her daughter and sent her to bed crying. Lori felt horrible. Needless to say, so did Katelyn.

Instead of offering her tips for redirecting power struggles, I asked, "Do you think Katelyn is in a power struggle, or is she just wanting to connect with you?" Tears welled up in Lori's eyes as she recognized and reinterpreted her daughter's "power struggles" as simply cries for attention and connection.

That night, Lori offered Katelyn some choices about a new bed-time routine. Katelyn chose to fall asleep in Mom and Dad's bed. Lori explained that after she fell asleep, they would carry her back to her bed. Instantly, the bedtime "power struggles" were replaced with a happy, peaceful, connected bedtime.

Get in the habit of asking yourself *Is this child's misbehavior really a cry for attention?* If it is, offer connection. After all, your child will not likely say, "Hey, Mom, I really need some quality time with you. Do you think you could check your Daytimer and schedule some one-on-one time with me?" It's up to you to take the lead.

Here are two stories about moms who successfully answered the call:

Julie was in the shower and Marcus, her four-year-old son, came upstairs whining and upset, crying.

She asked, "What's wrong, Marcus?"

"I want *you!*" he answered.

Julie was in a hurry to get ready for work and said some things she hoped would soothe him and get him to go back and play. It didn't work. She was directing him to "go there," not "come here." She then remembered the power of connecting and stopped her shower, donned a towel, picked him up, and held him on her lap. Within 30 seconds he scrambled down and went back to play. She finished her shower in peace and left for work with no further outbursts from her son. She experienced first-hand the parenting truth that it often takes less time to connect than it does to shoo your child away with your words.

My friend Karen gets the reward for the fastest response time in recognizing the call. We'd been talking on the phone for a few minutes when I heard her two-year-old start to scream hysterically. "Is she hurt?" I asked. "No, she wants Mommy's attention." Karen had left Tori's side and walked into another room to find some papers for me when Tori "lost it." She immediately recognized her child's meltdown as a call to connect. We hung up in the middle of the phone conversation. ". . . Talk to you later, bye!"

Karen called back about 30 minutes later to relate her success: After she'd gotten off the phone, she sat down on the floor and connected with Tori. Shortly after that, it was time for Tori to go with her babysitter for a play date at her friend's home nearby. When it came time to say "goodbye," Tori cried and screamed for Mommy. Karen told the sitter to "standby" and ignored the ringing phone as she sat back down and played with Tori for several minutes. She let go of her expectation about Tori going to the play date. When the sitter came back about 15 minutes later to see if Tori now wanted to go on the play date, Tori jumped up and said, "Bye, Mommy!" and ran out the door.

Almost without exception, we create more peace in the long run when we recognize the call to connect then take a few minutes to meet the child's *PHIL* needs.

THE SECOND MOVE: PRACTICE HIGH LEVEL CONNECTING EVERYDAY

The word *adore* means to worship or honor as a deity or as divine. *Cherish* means to hold dear, feel or show affection for, to keep or cultivate with care and affection. When we cherish and adore our children, treating them divinely, they begin to behave that way.

At the same time, learning to connect to your children is one of those powerful practices that's "simple but not easy." Simple, because you can learn how in minutes; not easy, because you may have to change lifelong habits to make this your automatic mode, your way of life, and you can if you're committed to Parenting with Soul. You can experience three levels of presence with your child. In order to spend most of your time at the highest level, it's helpful to be able to recognize the less-than-optimal levels. The levels are:

Low-Level Connecting: At this level, you're "there, but not there." Your physical body might be in the room. You may even be hugging your child or holding him on your lap, but your mind is miles away thinking things like *Did I remember to put dog biscuits on the grocery list? How do I want my hair cut tomorrow? Did I put the milk back in the fridge?*

I felt so proud to be an "at-home mom." By gosh, I was going to be there to give my child plenty of love and attention. One day, when one of my daughters was about three years old, she walked up to me in the early afternoon and I noticed green stuff oozing from her eyes. Pinkeye. My child had a nasty case of pinkeye and I had not made enough eye contact with her in the preceding six hours to see the glassy, bloodshot eyes, or to notice her rubbing her eyes and tap into her low energy. *Ouch!* A classic low-level connection.

Medium-Level Connecting: At this mid-level of connecting, you're "there with your agenda." You may be quite present, but you're not open to the possibilities because you already have a goal in mind. Some activities that constitute a medium-level connection include shopping, driving, going to a movie, lecturing, interrogating, running errands, and doing various family activities planned by the parents.

Medium-level connecting is certainly an improvement over low-level connecting and many medium-level activities are great fun. Also, many medium-level connecting activities, like grocery shopping with your child or driving them somewhere, are absolutely necessary. I'm not at all suggesting that you abandon these types of activities. The problem happens when we mistake medium-level connection for high-level connection. Medium-level connecting does not usually *PHIL* the four emotional needs. High-level connecting does. Also, with a little awareness on our part, medium-level activities can be bumped up to a higher level. For example, if the car needs to get washed, we can treat this as a chore or make it an interactive family project.

High-Level Connecting: In the strongest level of connecting, you are "there with *their* agenda." You're fully present, making the current moment the most important thing on *your* agenda. If you want a strong relationship with your child and the rich rewards that closeness brings, connect at this high level as often as possible. I doubt that any parent can operate in high-level connecting mode all the time. I certainly can't. However, we can all benefit by noticing how often we do manage to create this level of connecting. Depending on the age of your child, aim to connect at this level several times a day. Infants will require much more of this type of connection, while your preteen may seem to want no part of you but is still in great need of your presence in her life.

THE KARAOKE MACHINE: THREE LEVELS OF CONNECTING

Here's an everyday example of how the same event can lead to very different levels of connection:

Low-Level Connecting: You buy your children a karaoke machine for Christmas with the thought that maybe this will be one of those gifts that keeps the kids busy for long stretches of time. Your spouse and you agree to put it in the basement during the Christmas party, hoping it will keep the kids "out of your hair."

Medium-Level Connecting: You buy your children a karaoke machine for Christmas with the thought that they will really enjoy it. They ask you to help them set it up a few times and though you mean well, after putting the turkey in the oven, you get on the phone with a party guest and lose yourself in a discussion about the 30 ingredients you had to buy to make Martha Stewart's Christmas cookies. You do find time to at least unpack the machine for the kids and toss them the instruction manual. Later in the day, they sing a song for the Christmas guests. The adults all clap for the kids' performance.

High-Level Connecting: You buy your children a karaoke machine for Christmas with the thought that you will have a great time connecting as a family. The children ask you to come help them set up the machine. You agree to join them as soon as you put the turkey in the oven. After you finish with the turkey, you reluctantly let go of the idea of preparing those 30-ingredient cookies and instead go into their room and enthusiastically say, "Let's set up that karaoke machine." Together you read the instructions and assemble the machine. You hear the phone ring and though it's tempting to run and pick it up, you think *It can wait. I want to connect with the children for a few minutes right now.*

Each child sings a song, then you take a turn. Even though you're tone deaf, you belt out a few lines of "Twinkle, Twinkle Little Star." After watching a few more rounds, you say, "This was fun. The turkey's calling me now."

REACH FOR MORE HIGH-LEVEL CONNECTING

If you want to feel more connected to your child, add more high-level connecting moments to your day. Begin by stopping a few times each day to simply observe your connection level. Remember, noticing and accepting are an essential part of the change process. Then, make an effort to add more high-level moments using the eight steps for Moving Toward Your Child with Love from the previous chapter. Let go of perfection. Adding just one or two more high-level moments each day will transform your relationship with your child. You might want to keep a log for a week to become more conscious of how often each day you experience high-level connecting.

THE THIRD MOVE:
INVITE YOUR CHILD TO
"COME HERE," NOT "GO THERE"

The inspiration for this third move came to me during one particular week when I heard two very different stories that reminded me to actively reach out to my children.

One Tuesday, my nine-year-old daughter came home from playing at her friend's house (also nine-years-old) and said, "Mom, did you know that Amber's mom doesn't even read her a story at bedtime anymore, or lie with her?"

"She doesn't?" I asked, "I wonder why not."

"I don't know, but Amber says her mom doesn't want to be with her. If she comes out of her room, her mom says, 'Get back in your room and go to sleep.' When I told her that you and Dad tell us a story and lay with us, she said, 'You're *so* lucky!'"

Children rarely ask for the connection that they crave. It's up to us to anticipate their need to connect and meet it.

A few days later while teaching the weekend personal growth seminar, I met a mother of two teenage boys who was attending the course. At a break, I asked her about her relationship with her sons (ages 16 and 18). She said they were very close. "What's your secret?" I asked. "I read them bedtime stories every night until they were both in ninth grade," she replied. "Wow, that's your secret?" I asked. She shared that bedtime was the only time in the day that they could find to have uninterrupted quiet time. She said that it was only at this time, too, that her sons spilled their concerns and worries. "How did you decide to stop reading to them in ninth grade?" I asked. "Oh, they asked me," said the mother.

I made some powerful decisions after talking with that mother. First, I decided I want to be able to say that I have a close, connected, open relationship with my teenagers. Second, I committed to be present with my daughters for a bedtime story until they ask me to leave. In fact, I committed to being with them in a number of different activities, like walking them into their classroom or staying with them at birthday parties until they ask me not to.

A few years earlier, I realized that bedtime had become one of my least favorite times of the day and had been for quite a while. My two daughters were not necessarily fighting and resisting; it was just that the routine was taking 45 minutes to an hour, which left me feeling exhausted and disconnected. By the time I started their story, I felt too tired to be loving and fun.

One particularly difficult night, I left the children crying as I went to my room instead of lying with them. *How can I connect with them and shorten the bedtime routine so I'm not so depleted every night?* I pondered. *What do they want?* Connection, of course. I realized I'd been barking orders from the kitchen in an attempt to finish the dishes *while* orchestrating the bedtime routine. No mindfulness here. I'd been trying to do two things at once.

So, I let go of doing the dishes, cleaning the house, and trimming the bonsai and began a practice I call "come here," not "go there." At the beginning of the bedtime routine, I planted myself in my children's bedroom. They naturally gravitated toward me (just as they had when I was in the kitchen). Since connection was their primary objective and I was available, they prepared for bed in less than half the time they had been taking. And, as a bonus, I had more energy to connect with them.

Children want more than anything to be with you and to have your undivided attention. The younger they are, the more they want and need it. We're often quick to send them away (especially the more competent and independent they become): "Go clean your room." "Go get dressed." "Go brush your teeth." When we replace the word, "Go," with "Let's go" (even a few times each day), brushing teeth and getting ready for bed cease being a chore and become, instead, another opportunity to connect with Mom or Dad.

Practicing "come here," not "go there" means resisting the temptation to consistently send our children away to complete a task just because we know they are capable of doing something on their own. It means taking the time to connect by choosing to accompany our children more often than sending them away.

The "go there" habit results from a thought pattern that sounds something like *How can I get rid of the kids so I can have some peace and quiet?* I remember as a child, we would often visit another family at their home. The adults would almost always be upstairs and the children in the basement playing. One day, I walked into the kitchen where the adults were talking and the mother said, "What are you doing up here, get back downstairs and play." The underlying message when we practice "go there" is: "You are not wanted."

My husband and I unintentionally sent a similar message one night during the bedtime routine. We were both very tired and though we usually enjoyed putting our children to bed, we just wanted the night off. My nine-year-old came into the living room where Joe and I were seated and said, "Mom, Dad, come read to us." "You go," Joe said to me. "No you go," I said. I turned in time to see tears welling up in my daughter's eyes as she slinked off to her room. *Ouch!* Even though Joe and I were acting out of exhaustion, my child heard it as, "You are not important to me." Those kinds of messages can stay with us for a lifetime.

The remedy is to get in the habit of this kind of self-talk: *I know my child can do this alone, but could I strengthen our relationship by participating with him?* For example, my daughter plays the guitar and practices alone most of the time. And she is happy to do that. I started to join her for some of her practices. What a wonderful opportunity to be in her presence.

I'm not suggesting you set a goal to always practice "come here." Like high-level connecting, adding one or two "come heres" each day strongly connects you to your child. What's important is to balance your "come heres" with your "go theres" in a way that encourages your child. It can be just as discouraging to feel babied as to feel abandoned.

Here are some specific ways to change the "go there" habit with your words:

Instead of . . .	Try Saying . . .
"Why don't you walk the dog?"	"Let's take Rover for a walk."
"Go brush your teeth."	"I'll brush my teeth with you." (I put my toothbrush in the kids' bathroom for this one.)
"Go practice the piano."	"Can I watch you practice?"
And for the ultimate . . . "Go clean your room." "	"Let's go clean your room." or "Would you like some help cleaning your room?"

Your youngest child will be packing her bags and leaving for college or her first apartment sooner than you think. Your son's desire to be with his peers in the teen years will be here before you know it. If you are committed to developing and maintaining a rich and meaningful connection with your child, adopting the mindset of "come here," not "go there" will pave the way.

THE FOURTH MOVE: PUT CONNECTION BEFORE LOGISTICS

The logistics of parenting and contemporary life can feel over-whelming. As orchestraters of the morning, mealtime, and bedtime routines, not to mention homework, play dates, soccer practice, and more. We are busy! Parents often facilitate hundreds of happenings each day.

One way to greatly ease the stress of daily mechanics is to practice *connecting before logistics*. Morning is often the most intense part of my day. My children catch a very early bus and must complete a long list of "to dos" to make it out the door on time: pack lunch, get dressed, eat breakfast, put their coats on, etc. I began to notice that many days, the kids left on a tense note, which left me feeling stressed and disconnected. Most of the time there was not a big disconnect, just an undercurrent of disconnection. I realized that I was modeling stressful mornings, when what I really wanted was to show my children how to peacefully experience even the mundane parts of life.

I asked myself the all-important question: *What can I do to create more peace in the morning?* The answer was to connect first. As a result, my morning practice is to connect with my children before I utter one word about logistics. Before that, of course, I connect with my Source before I come downstairs (my favorite way to do this is by being in silence). Then I walk into my children's room, give them a hug and a kiss, make loving eye contact, and say, "Good morning." This takes all of ten seconds yet sets an incredibly loving and connected tone for the morning. Only after I have connected to each child do I say things like, "Time to eat breakfast . . . pack your homework . . . brush your teeth." When I practice connecting before logistics, mornings run exceptionally well! My children are much more likely to cooperate and I feel calmer and more connected all day long.

Most people seem to put logistics before connecting. When we make logistics more important than connecting, we contribute to the SAD epidemic sweeping our culture. I took my seven-year-old to the doctor with a fever of 103° F. A nurse I had never met swept into the waiting room and greeted us by saying, "Are you Alexa? Come this way. Put your coat down and get on the scales. I need to weigh you." No "hello," no "how are you," no eye contact, no smile. We were greeted with commands and a rushed attitude. My child, who was already feeling disconnected because she was sick, was now even more disconnected. I was upset. Probably without even knowing, this nurse committed a major customer service and connecting "no-no."

I once attended a birthday party for a six-year-old and noticed that, as each mom arrived to pick up her child, she greeted the mother of the birthday girl before greeting her own child. In several cases, the child would try to get her attention and the mom would tell the child not to interrupt. What kind of message does that give the child? That she's not important. In his book, *First Things First,* Stephen Covey reminds us that life is more likely to turn out the way we want if we focus on those activities that are "important and not urgent." Use any urgency as a reminder to stop and decide what's most important at this moment. One practical way I apply this to my life, which greatly eases the stress of daily mechanics, is to practice *connecting before logistics.*

With this fresh on my mind, several days later as I went to day-care to pick up my six-year-old, I made a special effort to connect with her first thing. Within seconds, Pam arrived. She and I had been playing phone tag for days, planning a school picnic. "Vickie!" she shouted hurrying toward us. It took every bit of self-control to stay focused on my child, but I did. Connection before logistics—or friends.

Prayer/Affirmation

I recognize and respond to the call to connect and as a result
I feel better and my relationship with my child flourishes.

Soulful Reminders

- **Recognize the call to connect**
- **Practice high level connecting everyday**
- **Invite your child to "come here, not go there"**
- **Put connection before logistics**

The Power of One Small Step

Write down one practice you learned or were reminded of in this chapter that you will use this week to make one of the four moves to a connected life. I started by kissing and hugging my children and making loving eye contact with them in the morning before speaking about logistics.

8

the seven deadly disconnects and their six second cousins

See everything;
overlook a great deal;
correct a little.

— POPE JOHN XXIII

Our ultimate connection skill is to buck lifelong habits and the strong cultural trends that encourage disconnection.

Standing in the video section of the market, I could clearly hear the animated conversation in the next aisle. A mother and her son were selecting a film together when a family friend approached them. The mother excitedly asked, "How are you? It's so good to see you!" Her friend enthusiastically replied, "Great. It's been such a long time!" Then turned to the boy.

"And how are you liking seventh grade?"

The mother replied, "He loves it, and he's so happy to be in middle school." The friend then noticed that the boy was wearing a football jersey and asked, "Do you play football?"

"Yes, he does," replied the mother, "and it's all we hear about every night at the dinner table. Football. Football. Football."

As I rounded the corner, I saw the dejected look on the boy's face as he shrugged off what seemed to be another in a series of failures to be heard. He was disappointed, discounted, and disconnected.

Talking for our children is just one of the subtle ways we damage our relationship and disconnect with them. All children want to be seen, heard, and connected with us.

We've looked at important ways to connect with our child. An equally important skill is recognizing the behaviors that disconnect us and that prevent the child from feeling *PHIL*ed. These behaviors aren't child-specific; they disconnect us in our business, and spiritual and personal lives as well. One day I mistyped "the feeling of joy" and it came out "the felling of joy." For you city dwellers, felling a tree means to cut it down. This began a reflection about the actions that cut down joy in our lives; they all had to do with disconnecting.

To connect to our child, we must be present physically, mentally, and emotionally. We must also buck lifelong habits and the strong cultural trends (like interrupting and talking for them) that encourage disconnection. Barriers to being fully present (and, therefore, connected) are myriad. Fortunately, the solutions are myriad as well. We just have to learn new responses. This list is by no means complete or the final word. In fact, I feel as if I'm barely doing these topics justice because they're at the heart of the SAD epidemic. There are books about some of these disconnects and parenting courses that can help you move beyond them. Check the resources section at the end of this book for materials that expand greatly on these topics.

Here are the seven greatest disconnects:

PHYSICAL ABSENCE

The Challenge

For a child to feel good about himself, we need to be physically present in his life. On the most extreme level, a child can feel abandoned and experience a physical disconnect when a parent dies, drops them off at an orphanage, is incarcerated, has a long hospital stay, or moves away as the result of a separation or divorce. A medium level of abandonment could take the form of long hours away from your children because of work, travel, or social engagements. We can also abandon our children physically when we're spending extended periods of time separately in the same house.

Before a speaking engagement in Denver, I was having my nails done at a hotel and a woman sitting near me asked where I was from and what I was doing there. When I told her that I was writing a book on parenting, she asked me to share the most important message from the book that she could apply to life as a single mother with a 15-year-old son. "Connect," was my response. "Oh, I know what you mean," she said. "My son's first basketball game was just last week and I showed up with flowers to congratulate him. No other parent did anything like that to acknowledge their son. Acknowledging them is so important and so few people take the time to show they care." I agreed.

A little bit later in the conversation she explained that she was starting a new business in a town five hours away and, thus, was out of town every week, Monday through Friday. "Who stays with your son?" I asked. "Oh, he is on his own," she replied. She must have sensed my concern. When she saw the look on my face, she retorted, "Oh, don't worry. I trust him completely. He's a great kid. Plus we have good quality time on the weekend."

I don't doubt that this woman's son is a great kid. I do doubt that this woman understands the vital importance of being involved in a child's life and that no amount of bouquets and weekend quality time makes up for time spent with your child. Her child is essentially alone. Ronald Levant, a psychologist at Harvard Medical School, agrees: "I think quality time is just a way of deluding ourselves in shortchanging our children. Children need vast amounts of parental time and attention. It's an illusion to think they're going to be on your timetable, and that you can say, 'Okay, we've got a half hour, let's get on with it.'"

I believe most parents love their children and the most common way they disconnect is by making other things—like providing financially, creating a comfortable home, or providing an array of enrichment opportunities—more important than connecting with their kids. In his book *Children: The Challenge,* Rudolf Dreikurs said, "Parents are so deeply concerned with providing the best for their children that they neglect to join them."

The Solution

Honestly assess the number of hours you spend with your children. For one week, keep track of the time you're physically with them. Whenever I've recorded some aspect of my life, like my spending or the foods I consume, I've surprised myself with what I've learned. If you realize you're not present with your child to the extent you want to be, brainstorm ideas with your spouse or get support from friends or a counselor.

HITTING

The Challenge

A minister approached me after a presentation in Atlanta to a conference of Christian families and said, "I gather you don't believe in spanking." I could tell from his tone that he had more than an academic interest. "That's right," I said. "I believe violence begets violence."

"Spare the rod and spoil the child!" he responded.

"Actually," I said, "The sheep were never hit with the rod by shepherds. The rod was used to *direct* the lead sheep." He disagreed and assured me that he makes sure he is not angry whenever he strikes his children. We were clearly poles apart in our philosophies and I felt uncomfortable with our exchange. This charming and charismatic 40-year-old, with an engaging smile, headed a growing church that was one of the most successful in its region.

Later that day in the conference hotel, I was sitting in the hot tub with a half dozen other mothers when a boy around six and a girl around four approached the water.

"Get in!" the boy told the girl. She dipped her toes in and pulled them out quickly. "It's too hot," she said.

"Get in!" he yelled.

"No!" she answered loudly.

"I said, get in!" he screamed, hitting her on the back of her head.

The girl began wailing as the boy screamed even louder, and began to spank her. "Get (whack), in (whack), right (whack), now!"

The other mothers and I sat in stunned silence at the sudden violence. Just as one of us stood up to intervene, the children's mother appeared, followed by her husband—the minister.

At age six, this boy had adopted the philosophy that spanking implies: If you can't get what you want when you want it, use physical force, especially if your target is smaller or weaker. Violence perpetuates violence.

The Solution

Adopt a form of discipline that connects you to your child. The books that appear in the resource section will point the way. The root word of discipline is the Latin word *disciplina,* which means *to teach by example.* Unfortunately, discipline has become associated with punishment and harsh actions. If you look up the word discipline, you'll also discover the obsolete meaning of the word— *guidance.* I invite you to resurrect the original meaning of discipline and begin to parent the way a great teacher instructs her followers—by offering guidance and a loving example.

The new definition of discipline in action connects you with your children and nurtures their spirit without compromising your wants and needs. It's the best of both worlds, and both worlds will feel more peaceful.

EMOTIONAL DISTANCING

The Challenge

We're not present emotionally if we're thinking of other things while our child is talking to us. We've also disconnected if we're thinking of what to say next, instead of listening. If we prejudge and decide what's so before interacting with our children, or don't feel interested in them or in what they're saying, they sense the loss of connection.

The state of your physical condition can also affect your emotional availability. Fatigue, whether it's caused by the ongoing stress of modern living, a too full schedule, physical illness, or sleep deprivation cuts the cord of connection. Likewise, hunger, illness, loneliness, or the distraction that comes from feeling upset all separate us on an emotional level from our child. Twelve-step programs have a guideline I like a lot called *HALT*: Don't get too *Hungry,* too *Angry,* too *Lonely,* or too *Tired.* It's good advice for all of us if we want to connect. E. Joseph Coleman affirmed the last of the HALT practices when he said, "The best bridge between despair and hope is a good night's sleep."

Feelings are the currency of connection, and many good-hearted and well-intentioned parents squander this rich part of life because they are simply not in touch with their feelings. This may be the result of their own childhood neglect or trauma or the family culture in which they were raised. Also, any addictions, including culturally sanctioned ones like overworking, disconnect us from our feelings and, therefore, from our child. Deepak Chopra states that, "When love is replaced by an object, the result is an addiction."

We may also disregard our child's feelings out of habit or because we want them to change. We may not take the time, as we make a decision that impacts the child, to anticipate his reaction. We may believe he'll conform to the feelings we expect, or assume we know his feelings when we don't. Even if the child expresses strong feelings, we may believe that the parent is boss and should prevail, or we may ignore them, hoping they'll morph into something we find more acceptable.

The Solution

Because there are so many reasons for emotional distancing, there's an array of solutions as well.

- **Speak with a Feeling Vocabulary: Get into the habit of saying, 'I feel . . .'' then finish it with one of these words: happy, angry, scared, sad, etc. Instead of saying, "You're late!" say, 'I feel angry that you didn't come home when you said you would." Or, perhaps more accurately, 'I felt scared when you didn't come home when you said you would."**

Feelings create connection, and this way of speaking has been painfully absent from many of our families of origin. I know that I've asked a lot of you in a few short paragraphs, but here's why it's so important:

On several occasions, a father with young boys will approach me after I teach the "feelings" part of the parenting program and say something like: "Vickie, if I do all this 'touchy-feely' stuff with my sons, won't I just raise my sons to be weak?" Dr. John Gottman, author of *Raising an Emotionally Intelligent Child,* answers this common concern. He conducted extensive longitudinal research on children and discovered many characteristics of what he refers to as emotion-coached children. These children:

- **Are better at focusing attention**

- **Relate better to other people, even in tough situations like getting teased in middle school**

- **Are better at understanding people**

- **Are better in school situations that require academic performance**

- **Have fewer infectious diseases**

Handling feelings also develops empathy and possessing the ability to empathize has been proven to be the number one deterrent to violence, especially murder.

What more compelling reasons could you find for helping your child get in touch with his feelings? We will explore the practice of acknowledging feelings more in depth in Chapter Ten: Hear Your Soul's Messages.

- *Nurture Thyself:* **We are able to be emotionally present when our needs are being met. Get in the habit of checking in with yourself and meeting your needs before you reach a crisis level. See the importance of consistently meeting your needs as a parent and anticipate them whether it is the need for food or a night out with friends.**

- *Heal Thyself:* One of the most important steps in becoming emotionally present is to do what it takes to heal the feeling of disconnection we experienced as children. It would be best if you could do this by next Tuesday. I joke here because I know what it takes to trek that path. It has taken me 15 years of conscious effort, and almost losing a loved one to alcoholism, to wake up and heal the pattern of shutting down feelings that were prevalent in our home and in so many others. Do whatever it takes to heal the past so you can move through the future with your child in a more connected way.

CONTROLLING

The Challenge

When we attempt to control another, we disconnect from our Higher Selves and from the person we are interacting with. This may possibly come as a surprise, but we truly can't control other people, places, or things. We can only control ourselves, and we're not always successful doing that. In families, the effort to control can take the form of talking for our children when they can speak for themselves, having an inflexible agenda, yelling, punishing, and spanking.

Parents may also attempt to control by tying allowances, rewards, or even their expressions of love to certain desired behaviors on the part of their child. In addition, some of us attempt to control their feelings for us, and their assessment of us, as good parents.

The problem is that many of us enter into the role of parent with unresolved power issues from our childhoods. Most of us were overpowered as children, so overpowering is our natural response, especially when the stress is on. Also, if the only parenting model we had was a controlling one, we consciously or unconsciously assume that role. Our culture fully supports us in doing this, as well as in nearly every other disconnecting practice.

The Solution

As more people change their parenting styles, our culture will become connected and loving as well.

- **Look for opportunities to give your child a sense of control. Give them choices.**
    - ⟾ **Which dress do you want to wear to the party?**
    - ⟾ **Would you like a tuna sandwich or a cheese sandwich today?**
    - ⟾ **Do you want to brush your teeth first or wash your face first?**
    - ⟾ **Do you want Daddy to tuck you in or do you want me to?**

- **Attend a personal growth course that helps you understand your need for control and offers support during your change process.**

- **Consciously choose one small arena you typically control that you will let go of just for the day. Some ideas: the clothes your children (and spouse?) wear, the order of the daily routine, the cleanliness of any room, or your child's behavior in public.**

BEING TOO PERMISSIVE

The Challenge

Would you be surprised to learn that the angriest and most violent youth of today come from home environments that were overly permissive? Sometimes, in an attempt to balance our own experience of being overly controlled when we were children or simply because we don't know any better, we provide less structure and limits than our child needs. When we do not set limits, or do not enforce limits, children decide that we don't care.

A few years ago, I worked closely with a group of teenage girls in a personal growth weekend. At one of our follow-up meetings a 15-year-old girl shared her upset through heavy sobs: "I used to think my mom was so cool. A few months ago, she bought beer for my friends and me and got drunk with us. She did it a few more times after that. All my friends told me that I had the most awesome mom and that they wished their parents were like her. Then some heavy stuff started happening at school with drugs and fights and boys and I couldn't talk to my mom. She only wanted to be my friend and I really needed someone to give me adult advice. I really, really needed a mom, not a drinking buddy."

This girl echoed the pain that so many children feel and few can name or would share if they could—the sense of abandonment and low self-esteem felt when parents fail to get involved in their lives and set limits.

The Solution

Boundaries and specific guidelines, backed up with logical consequences for inappropriate behavior, provide a connection between our child and us, and also contribute to the child's sense of security in the world. For more information, read one of the *Positive Discipline* titles listed in the Resources section.

NEEDING TO BE RIGHT

The Challenge

Sometimes we get the idea that, as parents, we have all the answers simply because we have logged in more hours on the planet. This can take the form of needing to have the last word or to appear to be right, no matter what. And where does this need to be right come from? Usually from the strong message from our own parents that being right is more important than everything else. Use the right grammar. Get the right answer on math problems. Learn how the world works. As a result, we get the message that we are powerful when we are right and a failure when we are not.

A coaching client shared what Rudolf Dreikurs calls a "right vs. close" incident that happened when she was seven: She and her father went next door to see the neighbor's kittens. When she saw them she burst into a gleeful chant, "Look at the baby kittens, Daddy, look at the baby kittens!" Her father turned to her and in a stern voice said, "'Baby kitten' is redundant, the word kitten implies baby." It was at that point that she started containing her joy and self-expression, especially in front of her father. Thirty years later, she is attending personal growth courses and therapy sessions to reclaim her childish innocence and joy. After much work, she makes it a point to choose close over right with her children.

The Solution

Adopt a sense of inquiry and wonder. You'll model important skills for your child and take a lot of pressure off yourself (and your child). Aim to accept and readily share your mistakes. Feel comfortable saying, "I don't know." Resist the urge to correct minor mistakes at the expense of connection. This way the child thinks, *My parent doesn't have to be right all the time, neither do I,* while keeping connected. Gerald Jampolsky says it in a way I love: "Do you want to be right or do you want to be happy?"

Recently, Brianna told me she thought her spring guitar concert would be half an hour long. I was sure it would be longer, probably an hour, in order for all the kids to play. It did take an hour and as we walked out to the car, she said, "Hey, it's 8:20. It did take an hour." I didn't say anything but, "Mmm hmm." When we refrain from pointing out that we were right and our child was wrong, we bolster our child's self esteem and encourage her in expressing her perspective, opinions, and ideas—fundamental to thinking for herself—which becomes increasingly important as she enters her teen years.

THE BIG FOUR NEGATIVES: CRITICISM, WORRY, FEAR, AND GUILT

The Challenge

Think about it: Positive energy is forward moving, empowering, and ever expanding. Negativity constricts. Imagine your child as an energy soup. With every interaction, we make the broth weaker or more robust. Are you aware of what you add to the mix? All forms of negativity disconnect. Criticism, worry, fear, and guilt are among the most negative.

In my opinion, Dale Carnegie wrote the treatise on *criticism* when he said, "There's no such thing as constructive criticism. All criticism is destructive." Criticism of anyone or anything immediately cuts the ability to connect. Your child cannot feel close to you when she lives in fear of being criticized. Children who live with criticism often develop the belief that *What I do is never good enough*. This kind of limited thinking carries over into adult life and is why so many people hold themselves back from pursuing the life they want.

Whether we're fretting about our child or about world events, *worry* pops us into the future and out of the present, which is where connection occurs. I wondered for years why I disconnected from my mother during my teen years. She had been so loving and patient that my retreat (that lasted into my late twenties) didn't make sense. Recently I realized and shared with her that I backed off because when I brought a concern to her she added huge doses of paralyzing worry to the pot. "Therefore, do not worry about tomorrow, for tomorrow will worry about itself. Each day has enough trouble of its own." Mt 6:34

Fear, even when unspoken, acts as a damper on everyone's spirit. When we live in fear we hold ourselves back from a life of joy and pass this negative view that the world is unsafe on to our children. Fear also keeps us from making decisions. Napoleon Hill said, "It is a major indictment against our civilization that the vast majority of people keep most of their thought power centered on their fear, rather than on conceptions and deep beliefs which can bring them what they want."

Any *guilt* we may feel at being less than perfect parents prevents us from offering our child the perfect gift—our full presence.

The Solution

Replace these four negatives with forward moving practices. In Chapter Eleven: Attract What You Want, you will learn powerful tools to assist you in creating more of what you want by focusing on the positive.

THE SIX SECOND COUSINS

If you can clear up the Seven Deadly Disconnects, your family life will change dramatically. Minimizing the following six behaviors will help even more:

YELLING

The Challenge

We yell when we don't know what else to do. When we overpower and intimidate our child this way, our relationship suffers. When the relationship suffers, our chances of getting cooperation go way down, so we yell again and continue to feed the vicious cycle of disconnection. This wreaks havoc on the child's core need to feel *Powerful, Heard, Important,* and *Loved.*

The Solution

It's not enough to simply resolve to never yell again. Breaking out of the yelling habit takes strong desire and commitment. Remember to nurture yourself; this is the vital inner work. When we feel centered, we're naturally more resourceful and, therefore, more likely to choose a less destructive parenting method. Take a parenting class. You will get support and learn effective parenting skills to use instead of yelling. If you do yell, apologize. This teaches the child that the behavior is inappropriate and helps reconnect the two of you.

THREATS

The Challenge

Threats are not only ineffective; they are often harmful. Whether big or little, they disconnect. If we don't follow through with our threat, our children learn they can't trust us. When combined with yelling and hurtful words, threats pack a devastating blow.

The Solution

Offer consequences instead of threats. When your child misbehaves, hold her accountable using a respectful tone. Wait until you have calmed down to talk about an upset. Avoid using the word "never" (e.g., "You are never allowed to have a friend sleep over again."). We rarely mean it.

Instead of a Threat (and a Harsh Tone)	Use a Consequence (and Respectful Tone)
"Get down from the slide now or we'll never come to the park again."	"If you want to come back to the park and play, you need to get down from the slide when I ask."
"If you keep wiping the crumbs onto the floor, you can just clean the whole kitchen next time!"	"If you wipe the crumbs on the floor, you'll need to vacuum them up."
"If you don't bring me your dirty clothes on Mondays, you can do your own laundry."	"I will wash all the clothes that are in the basket by Monday."
"You are through using the car! I'm sick of always having be the one to fill it with gas."	"If you forget to put gas in the car, you will have to walk to school next week. You can try again the week after."

COMMANDS

The Challenge

As children grow older and more self-sufficient, our role begins to resemble a manager more than a caretaker. It's easy to revert to short commands to get the kids up and out the door on time. The only problem is that too many commands can disconnect us from our children.

Put yourself in your child's place for a moment. Imagine arriving at work to a barrage of (even friendly) commands: Hang your coat up, be sure to check your messages, come in my office. A full day of this kind of interaction would discourage most of us.

The Solution

It's okay to use commands, just don't overuse them. Try replacing commands with information and questions. This will minimize power struggles and improve your relationship. As a bonus, when we give information or ask a question, our child learns essential thinking skills. These two practices help a child to look within to process information instead of react.

Instead of a Command . . .	A Question . . .	And/or Information
"Put your shoes on." "Hurry up."	"What else do you need to do to get ready for the park?"	"You will need to wear sneakers to the park."
"Don't jump in that pool. You are too close to those people."	"What will it take to get to the party on time?" "What should you do before you jump in?"	"We need to leave in ten minutes." "You're very close to those people in the pool."

INTERROGATING

The Challenge

In an effort to connect, many well-meaning parents bombard their children with questions, especially after a separation. When we ask too many questions, we can inadvertently disconnect from our child. Intense interrogation can result in the child feeling pressured *(I have to come up with an acceptable answer)* and invaded *(My mom always has to know everything)* and whisks them out of the present moment. At the end of the day your toddler will struggle to recall the art project they worked on at 10:00 that morning. Remember that children live in the present moment. One day when Alexa was talking to her grandmother, she pulled the phone away from her ear and handed it to me, with a befuddled expression. When I asked her what was wrong, she said, "Grama asked me what I was doing. *I was talking to her.*"

Children feel sensitive to the nuances of communication. Is your intention to connect or simply extract information? Like commands, questions are nondirectional, not sharing control of the conversation, and not connecting.

The Solution

When reuniting with your child, use the eight steps to Move Toward Your Child with Love. Or, offer a simple greeting like, "It's nice to see you." Often being with your child in silence elicits the same amount of information.

INTERRUPTING

The Challenge

Children don't always form their ideas as swiftly as adults so we sometimes interrupt them. Think of each interruption as a scissors cutting the connection.

The Solution

When your child is talking, make friendly eye contact and breathe. Stay present. Take in the words, even if you think you know what she'll say. Keep the connection.

LABELS

The Challenge

Labels limit, even if they seem positive on the surface, and, like negativity, they restrict the flow that characterizes connection. Labels are intrinsically static and lock us into a moment of time instead of *being* in the moment. Telling a child he's a good boy is actually as constricting as saying he's a bad boy. Even such seemingly harmless labels as "nice," "good student," and "tattletale," leave a child feeling judged and disconnected.

I was talking with my mother on the phone one day while my

children played nearby. I shared with her how one of my daughters was a "spender" and the other was a "saver." I was not complaining, just passing along an observation. A few months later the daughter I had labeled a "spender" walked up to me and showed me that she had saved forty dollars. "See," she defended, "I'm not just a spender like you said to Grandma." I felt terrible when I realized how long she held on to the feeling of being judged. I had unintentionally placed her in a box and discouraged her.

When we compare our child to others, we're also labeling them in terms of what they're not and setting up an impossible task for them to be someone else.

The Solution

Avoid using labels of any kind. If you would like to change a behavior, *discuss* your feelings and desire for a change.

THE FALLACY OF "IT WORKED!"

Often parents come to class eager to share their most recent parenting success story inspired by the latest magazine article on child rearing. The conversation goes something like this: "Vickie, I tried this new 'thing' (time-out, spanking, counting to three, etc.), and it worked! Jill gets dressed when we tell her to now." They may add that Jill cried for three days, wet the bed, and quit speaking to them, but, by gosh, "It worked."

In these cases, "it worked" means the child did what the parents wanted them to do. If our goal is happy, healthy relationships with happy, healthy children, these techniques ultimately *don't work*. When parents apply spot solutions with little or no consideration for the long-term effect of this type of discipline on their relationship, this faulty thinking is like saying, "Vickie, no gas was available, so I just put water in my gas tank, and it worked. I've only driven three miles today, but, so far, so good!"

I challenge you to embrace a new definition of "it worked."

When you say "It worked," make sure you can answer "yes" to all three of these questions:

1. **Did the level of cooperation and peace increase?**

2. **Was my child's self-esteem enhanced?**

3. **Did I feel good afterward?**

When you can answer, "yes" to all three of these questions, you'll know you're parenting on higher ground. And, like an increasing number of parents, you'll begin to reap the long-lasting rewards of a close, connected relationship with your child: open communication, mutual respect, and more cooperation.

OUT OF THE MOUTHS OF TEENS

Several years ago I was invited to give a talk to a group of sophomores and juniors at the local high school. I mentioned that in a few hours I would be teaching my second night of the six-week parenting course on the topic of encouragement. I then asked them to offer anonymous words of guidance to these parents of small children. I specifically asked them to share the most discouraging things their parents did and to suggest what would have been more encouraging.

When I got to my car, I pulled out the papers, read them all, and sobbed. I was astonished by their openness in sharing their hurt. More than that, their suggestions for more encouraging responses exactly mirrored modern parenting philosophy. Their examples could have come out of a parenting textbook! They are in the order of frequency.

The Most Discouraging Things My Parents Did to Me	What Would Have Been More Encouraging
They yelled at me without a good cause. (yelling)	Listen to my side of the story. Speak to me with respect.
Hit me. (hitting)	Don't hit me. Explain what I did wrong. Respect me.
They said, "Why can't you be like your sister? She does her chores and doesn't complain!" (comparing)	They said, "We would appreciate it if you would do your chores without complaining."
"You are lazy/stupid/a problem/ a brat/selfish/spoiled/just like your mother." (labels)	See where I am coming from and treat me like an individual.
They use threats like, "I'm going to take away your stereo."	Talk it through.
They always think they are right. (needing to be right)	Talk to me on the same level. Stop talking down to me.
They told me to gain weight; that I look like an Ethiopian. (criticizing)	Keep their negative comments to themselves.

I read the responses to my class that night. Most of the parents cried, too. I carry those tattered pages with me and read them to every parenting class I teach and get the same response. These could be your children. These are your children coming back from the future to tell us what they want—connection.

So watch for the Seven Deadly Disconnects and Their Six Second Cousins as you move through your day. Notice which of these crop up to disconnect you. Once you discover something you want to change, search out the resources you need to help you become a catalyst to connection instead of a catalyst to disconnection.

Prayer/Affirmation

Help me to lovingly observe
the times I disconnect
from my child and You,
and redirect me
to connection.

Soulful Reminders

- **The Seven Deadly Disconnects are:**
    - ⟹ **Physical absence**
    - ⟹ **Hitting**
    - ⟹ **Emotional distancing**
    - ⟹ **Controlling**
    - ⟹ **Being too permissive**
    - ⟹ **Needing to be right**
    - ⟹ **Negativity in the form of criticism, worry, fear, and guilt**

- **Their Six Second Cousins are:**
    - ⟹ **Yelling**
    - ⟹ **Threats**
    - ⟹ **Commands**
    - ⟹ **Interrogating**
    - ⟹ **Interrupting**
    - ⟹ **Labels**

THE POWER OF ONE SMALL STEP

Write down one practice you learned or were reminded of in this chapter that you will use this week to catch yourself disconnecting. I started by noticing how I *felt* after an interaction with my child. If it felt bad for me, I realized it probably felt bad for her.

Principle #2

Awaken Your Intuition

9

summon
the
power
of
silence

It is those who have a deep and real inner life
who are best able to deal
with the irritating details
of outer life.

— EVELYN UNDERHILL,
BRITISH AUTHOR

Silence is the medium/lifeblood/life source of intuition. When my children were around the ages of three and six, I woke up one morning with laryngitis. Though I felt fine, my whispers were barely audible and I wondered how I could possibly orchestrate the happenings of the day with no voice. I've never lost my voice before or since, and that one day without it proved to be a huge gift.

That morning, after I came downstairs, I drew my children near and said, "Mommy cannot talk today (my six-year-old could barely contain her joy), so I need your help. You will need to pay extra attention when I ask you for something, okay?" They shook their heads in bemused agreement.

I was astounded at the level of cooperation, peace, and harmony that we experienced that day. I could not bark commands across the house. I could not bark commands, period. To preserve what was left of my voice I had to go *to* the children to get their attention. It was amazing for me to learn how very few commands and words are required to get through the day. As I reflected on this extraordinary experience, I realized I could bring the same peace and calm to days when I did have my voice, if I just didn't use it as much.

Over time, I explored the power of silence, specifically as it related to parenting. Thomas Keating was right when he said in *Open Mind, Open Heart,* "The deeper your interior silence, the more profoundly God will work in you without your knowing it." As I consciously added more moments of silence to my day, my intuition expanded, and life with the children became smoother. By infusing your days with silence, you can:

- **Reduce anxiety**

- **Gain clarity**

- **Get centered**

- **Connect with your Higher Self**

- **Connect with others**

- **Communicate with your children from a place of peace**

English astrologer Jonathan Cainer accurately describes our world today: "These days none of us gets left alone long enough with our most private thoughts and our deepest feelings. Always we are being urged to communicate. To express ourselves. To externalize. I wonder how much better life might be for everyone if it had a few more silent minutes in it?"

ESTABLISH YOUR SILENCE PRACTICE

There's no right way to do it. The goal is simply to find opportunities to be with yourself in silence, to let silence lead you to your most private thoughts and deepest feelings, to experience the peace that comes from temporarily halting the barrage of input from the information age, and to experience peace and connection.

When we regularly experience the soothing experience of silence, we create a well we can draw from when things get hectic. Try one or more of these practical ideas for cultivating silence in your life:

- **Take five minutes in the morning to sit in silence before joining your family**

- **Look for moments in your day when you can sit quietly for a few minutes**

- **Exercise in silence**

- **Take a walking meditation**

- **Do the dishes in silence**

- **Enjoy a meal in silence**

- **Turn off your car radio or stereo**

"Silence understood as no obligation for social discourse allows the conscious mind a respite," according to Joan R. Tarpley in *The Tao of the Goddess*. Parents in one of my classes at first resisted the idea of creating a silent practice. They did, however, reluctantly agree to try something small the next week. Each person chose a time of day or experience that made them feel stressed and chose to add silence. Here are some of their results:

Opportunity to Infuse a Moment with Silence	Result
While the baby is napping	"I felt more peaceful and rested when I stopped for a few moments instead of racing around the entire time."
While nursing	I felt more connected to my child.
In the shower	I got lots of creative ideas and felt more peaceful than I do when listening to the news.
On the way to pick up my child from daycare	I felt more calm and centered when I greeted him.

The calm place created by meditating or any other silence practice is the doorway through which you connect with your intuition and your child. We can only open the doorway when we feel calm and present, not when we feel anxious, stressed, or focused elsewhere. This is the power of practicing silence, which enhances our interactions with children in several specific ways.

SILENCE CREATES A VOID
THAT INVITES EXPRESSION

After hearing about the benefits of silence, Jenni, a mother of three, decided to silently connect with her oldest, six-year-old Eric, at bedtime. After reading him a bedtime story, she usually kissed him goodnight and left the room or stayed just a few minutes. One night she decided to stay an extra long time in silence. After about five minutes (which seemed like forever to her), the usually quiet, withdrawn, and shy Eric started talking about all the happenings at school that day. He shared as never before, telling details of life at school, friends, and his concerns about being teased by one of the older boys.

When we inject some silence into our experiences with our children, they are likely to fill the void with closely held information. I've seen it again and again in my home and with other parents. You may feel astonished to see, often for the first time, glimpses of your child's inner life.

Cheryl had a similar experience with her six-year-old son Matt. They were lying in bed one morning and she chose to interject long silent pauses into their conversation.

Matt: I'm sick.

(Silence)

Cheryl: Do you want a cough drop?

Matt: I hate school.

(Silence)

**Matt: I don't actually hate school.
It's just that my friends are mean.**

(Silence)

Cheryl: That doesn't feel very good, does it?

**Matt: Actually, if I don't go to school, I get to see Dad.
(His father worked nights.)**

Again, it was the silence that invited the expression of strong feelings. She also acknowledged his feelings about missing his dad, which opened the communication lines even more.

SILENCE HONORS THEIR PACE

"Hurry up." "Come on." "Let's go." Children are often at the mercy of our hectic pace. If we can even sometimes allow them to set the pace we bless them greatly. I accidentally learned the lesson on the power of silence and honoring my child's pace. One day I had a severe migraine yet really needed to go to the grocery store. As the headache receded, I packed up my four-year-old and took off. As I entered the store, the fluorescent lights reactivated the headache. I moved very slowly (speed would also exacerbate things) down the aisles, gathering the essentials.

As we rounded a corner, Alexa spotted a tower of colorful balls. "I want to play with a ball!" she exclaimed. My usual response would have been, "No, we have to go." Instead, beaten down by the pain, I simply handed her a ball and stood holding my head, leaning against the cart. After about a minute, she said, "Okay. We can go." *After one minute? I argued with her all those others times, when all she required was one minute?* I learned.

Now more on purpose with my practice, I look for opportunities to honor my child's pace whenever possible. Recently I pulled into a store parking lot and turned to the back seat. Usually I park, open the door, and coax the kids out with, "Come on, girls. Let's go." But as I looked back, I noticed they had spread their money out on the back seat and were stacking and counting it. I took the opportunity to sit in silence until they finished. Again, it took less than one minute to infuse our experience with some calm, peace, and connection.

SILENCE: THE ESSENTIAL LISTENING SKILL

When you rearrange the letters in the word L-I-S-T-E-N, you get S-I-L-E-N-T. Good listening requires silence. Wait for the child to finish before you respond. Resist the temptation to interject or interrupt. Use the silence to quiet your own mind's wanderings as your child is speaking.

THE S-O-U-L PROCESS FOR CONNECTING WITH YOUR CHILD

Rita Weiss, Professor Emerita, Speech, Language, and Hearing Sciences, at the University of Colorado in Boulder, along with some of her students, developed a method (the S-O-U-L Process) for helping adults understand how to communicate more effectively with children and to create classrooms where children would naturally communicate among themselves while working together. The training program came to be called INREAL.

The S-O-U-L Process

- *S* stands for Silence. Instead of talking, you see yourself as the "silent joyful facilitator" of this connection.

- *O* means Observe. Quiet your thoughts and look. Follow your child's lead rather than impose your agenda or opinions.

- *U* reminds us that the only goal here is to Understand what our child wants in the moment and that our child's deepest need is connection.

- *L* means Listen.

Silence, Observation, Understanding, and *Listening* do not happen independently. You listen when you observe; you observe when you listen. You are silent in observing and listening. You understand during and after listening, observing, and being silent. Approaching your child in the spirit of S-O-U-L helps you to connect in a meaningful way.

INFUSE YOUR INTERRUPTIONS WITH SILENCE

"Excuse me. *Excuse me!*" Have you ever witnessed a child who has learned the polite words to say but not the polite tone to use when interrupting? My children learned a lovely skill for getting their preschool teacher's attention without interrupting or shouting, "Excuse me!" The teacher asked the children to place a hand on her shoulder (quietly and gently, no tapping or poking) if they needed her while she was working with another student. In return, she agreed to acknowledge them by placing her hand on theirs (that way they feel *Heard*). She would turn to talk with them at the earliest break in her conversation with the other student. This classroom, at a Montessori school, was perhaps the most peaceful I have seen. We adopted the practice at our home for both the parents and children and it continues today. The primary agreement is for the child to be gentle and the parent or teacher to respond quickly. It works like a charm!

One night my daughters each invited friends to sleep over. Both guests had been in the same Montessori classroom. I was turned away from the girls talking on the phone when suddenly I felt four hands on my back. I turned to see four smiling faces anxious to ask me a question. At the first opportunity, I took a moment to answer their question. What a joy to be with children who had learned such an appropriate way to get their needs met. Also, they really appreciate it when they receive the same respectful practice from their parents.

Another way I have taught my children to peacefully get their needs met if I am on the phone is by writing a note to me. (Part of my commitment to Parenting with Soul is that I'm rarely on the phone when my children are home. If you spend a large amount of time on the phone instead of connecting with your children, this practice will lose its effectiveness.) My children heartily adopted my value of silent interruptions. One day our tenant, who lives over our garage, came to the door while I was on the phone, asking to speak with me. "You can't interrupt her," said my five-year-old, "she's on the phone. You'll have to write a note." A few seconds later my tenant handed me a note that read *The washer is on fire!* Later we discussed safety exceptions for silent interruptions.

PEACEFUL REQUESTS

I was eating lunch at the high school football field where a dozen kindergartners from a nearby Waldorf school were running around. When it was time to go, their teacher stood in the end zone and with a friendly silence waved her arms up and down in a V, like someone guiding a plane into the gate, motioning the kids toward her. As each child spotted her, they nudged a friend and ran toward her. Some were more reluctant than others, yet within minutes, all the children joined her. I'm certain it took less time and energy for her to silently round up those children than it would have yelling across the field. Also, teacher and children felt good after the interaction.

When negotiating, making a proposition, or answering a question for your child, pause for a moment of silence:

"No, you may not sleep over at Molly's house tonight." *Silence*

"You need to wear shoes in the store." *Silence*

"If we get into the car by 2:00, we'll have time to stop by the playground on the way to the Cub Scout meeting." *Silence*

In sales this is known as the "silent close" and can feel uncomfortable at first, especially for those of us raised in word-ridden western society. Here is the secret of the silent close: Whoever speaks first after the proposal is offered will make a concession in the negotiation. So make the proposal, then zip your lip.

INVOKING A MAGIC MINUTE OF SILENCE

I was standing at the checkout counter talking with the cashier and writing a check for the groceries when, for the umpteenth time, my children approached and bombarded me with questions (yes, they had temporarily forgotten the "hand on the shoulder" technique). I was overwhelmed with the incoming data and snapped at the girls, "I need peace and quiet right now, dammit!" They sulked away. I felt bad. As we walked to the car, I apologized. Later, I wondered how I could find a more appropriate way to more lovingly set a limit in those situations.

I had a watch with a one-minute timer on it; hence, the magic minute. The magic minute is a way for anyone to ask for a minute of silence when they feel overwhelmed or just need a minute of peace. Except in cases where talking is absolutely necessary (e.g., the washer is on fire), anyone can ask, anytime. I then hit the timer button on my watch and everyone remains silent for a minute. The key is to ask for your minute in a friendly tone. Also, if you want to try this, set it up when things are peaceful. Then, when things heat up, you already have a group agreement in place. We have dramatically shifted the energy of some negative situations using the magic minute. Here are times *you* might want to use the magic minute:

- **In the car with noisy children and you need to intensely concentrate (e.g., bad weather, traffic jam, unfamiliar terrain)**

- **When your child is asking emphatically for something and you need time to think. If we answer, 'Pleeeaase, can we go?' with, 'I'd like a minute of silence," kids** learn three things: 1) To respect other people's need to take time to process information; 2) How to take care of themselves; 3) How to create more peace and calm

• Anytime you want to shift the energy of a situation

Your child may also want to ask for a magic minute of silence in various situations. Be sure to respect their request and even prime them with these possibilities:

• When they are gathering their thoughts in a discussion

• When you and your spouse are arguing

• When you lose your temper

• When they are trying to fall asleep in the car

• If you are talking excessively

REDUCE ENVIRONMENTAL OVERLOAD

Noisy environments, such as TV, cell phones, radios, or a blaring stereo provide little space to feel connection or to hear those intuitive whispers. We are either the master or the servant to technology. Try turning off your cell phone, TV, and radio for short intervals during the day and bask in the stillness. Dinnertime is more connecting for everyone when you minimize these distractions.

Mary Manin Morrissey offers insight and an inspiring solution to the television dilemma: "Psychologists have found that the most often spoken words in the average American family's home are 'What's on?' and 'Move over.' Think about it. The most cherished possession in the American home is the remote control. And if it gets lost, we create great drama, pulling apart couch cushions until the prized possession is again in sight. Consider taking a media fast. Turn off the television and radio for a week and revel in the stillness."

If turning off your TV for a week is too much, start small by turning it off during mealtimes or during the morning and bedtime routines. Many a coaching client has discovered that getting a toddler to bed is much easier when the television is off. The appeal is often too much for them to resist and leaves them feeling like they are missing the party in the living room. Take moments of silence to listen and deepen your communication with your Creator. Learn to listen to the sound of your soul.

SUBSTITUTE SILENCE FOR EXCESSIVE TALKING

If we talk constantly, we're not open to the two-way experience of connection. As the Japanese proverb says, "Speech is silver, silence is golden." Look for opportunities in your day to fill with silence. Become what Abraham-Hicks calls a silent, joyful orchestrater, or as Max Ehrman says, "Go placidly amid the noise and haste and remember what peace there may be in silence." Here are some of my wordless interactions:

- Alexa dipped the sleeve of her shirt in cream cheese at the bagel store, from her elbow to her wrist. She showed me her sleeve and I peacefully dipped a napkin in water and cleaned her sleeve.

- I started putting my children's lunch boxes on the stairs to the door instead of telling them 20 times not to forget their lunch boxes.

- Alexa gets into the car with messy hair, and as I'm driving I just hand her a hairbrush (as a bonus, my choice of no words also greatly minimized this month-long power struggle over brushing her hair before going to preschool).

- Brianna sneezes. I just hand her a tissue.

In the words of Haim Ginott, "What you can say in a paragraph, say in a sentence. What you can say in a sentence, say in a word. What you can say with a word, say in a gesture."

THE NEW AND IMPROVED SILENT TREATMENT

We've all experienced silence that connects and silence that disconnects. The difference is your intention. One of my friends grew up in a family where the mother gave the silent treatment to the father and barely spoke to the children when the parents had an argument. One Christmas, the mother didn't speak to anyone for four days because she was disappointed with her gift.

Most of us are probably more familiar with cold, disconnecting silence than the friendly silence that "seldom doth harm," at least according to the anonymous creator of this saying. We've experienced stunned silence, confused silence, and numb silence, but for most of us, friendly silence will be a new experience, bringing new rewards. I read recently in *New Age Magazine* about a new recording artist who's taking Europe by storm, Deva Premal, from Germany, who sings devotional songs. Her trademark is no clapping. The audience simply basks in the positive energy after each song.

Since ancient times, silence has been worshipped as an important part of many spiritual disciplines. When we make it a part of our parenting discipline, we intensify loving connections with our children. "With practice, silence is no longer passive but dynamic, something with energy that stays with us and guides us throughout the day," states Wayne Simsic in *Praying with Meister Eckhart*.

Prayer/Affirmation

Silence paves the way
for peaceful interactions
with my Self and my children.

Soulful Reminders

- By infusing your days with silence, you can:
    - ⟹ Reduce anxiety
    - ⟹ Gain clarity
    - ⟹ Get centered
    - ⟹ Connect with your Higher Self
    - ⟹ Connect with others
    - ⟹ Communicate with your children from a place of peace

- There's no right way to have a silence practice. Simply find opportunities to be with yourself in silence.

- Silence is an essential listening skill that creates a void, which invites expression, and also honors your child's pace.

- Infuse your requests and interruptions with silence.

THE POWER OF ONE SMALL STEP

Write down one practice you learned or were reminded of in this chapter that you will use this week to bring more silence into your life. I started by silently getting my children's attention by placing my hand on their shoulder.

10

hear your soul's messages

When we learn to parent more from our hearts and less from our heads, we naturally do what's best for our children (and for us), and that's what intuitive parenting is all about. My own failure to trust my intuition, in favor of advice from the "experts," resulted in one of my most devastating parenting experiences. When my older daughter was two, she began having difficulty going to sleep each night. We had moved into a new home and though she had previously gone to bed and slept through the night with ease, she was now up several times each night wanting to get into bed with us. *Getting* her to sleep each night was next to impossible. "Mommy, come lie with me some more—just one more minute."

Understandably, she felt upset. Her whole world had been turned upside-down in the process of the move. I was struggling, too. I was seven months pregnant, desperately in need of sleep, and this nightly production was *really* wearing on me. So, I did what so many good parents do. I bought a book by the current parenting "expert" about getting your child to sleep through the night.

I followed the author's advice to a "T." After all, *he* was a doctor. The plan was to let my child "cry it out" to some extent. I was to sit by her bed the first night to get her to go to sleep. Each successive night, I was instructed to move farther and farther away from her, ending up, on the fourth and final night of the plan, outside her bedroom with the door closed. On that fourth night, I was outside the bedroom door holding it shut as my child screamed and pounded on the door, begging and pleading to do the most natural thing in the world—be with her mommy.

I will never forget my child's hopeless cries coming from the other side of that door. I will never forget the gut-wrenching agony as I faithfully followed the "expert's" advice—all the while, ignoring my inborn, powerful, and exceedingly accurate guidance system—my intuition. Did the sleep plan "work"? You bet it did. The author said that the child would learn appropriate sleep patterns in four to five nights, and she did.

I felt, however, that in the process I had also killed her spirit.

Mine, however, had ripped wide open. As I lie in bed that fourth night, crying myself to sleep, I knew I had done something terribly wrong. I had forgotten to listen. I had allowed myself to become so disconnected from my soul, that I ignored the warning bells going off inside me.

Here's the good news: I never again ignored my intuition like I did on that fateful fourth night. The even better news: My daughter survived this and other early disconnected parenting tactics. Not only did she survive; she continues to thrive. Ten years later, she's a very happy, healthy, loving child with loads of self-confidence and joy oozing from her being. I feel convinced that one reason she is happy and healthy today is because I started listening to my intuition.

I didn't stop buying books by the parenting experts. I don't recommend that you stop buying the books either. In fact, I bought more books. What I'm recommending is that you choose a book, a daycare, a doctor, or anything for your child only after you have consulted your inner self.

BECOMING AN INTUITIVE PARENT

When I say "intuition," I mean that part of us that's wiser and more knowing. *Webster's* defines intuition as the ability to perceive or know things without conscious reasoning. As Ernest Holmes affirms in *The Science of Mind,* "Today I directly experience the reality of Spirit, allowing It to renew my mind, guide my decisions, and direct my affairs." Intuition is also referred to as our higher self, our inner being, gut instinct, a sixth sense, soul. I am not suggesting that we abandon "conscious reasoning." Use both intuition *and* conscious reasoning and reap the amplified rewards of intuitive parenting. If we learn to hear and follow our inner guidance, we'll dramatically reduce the level of stress in our lives and in our families. We will:

- **Feel confident about our parenting choices**

- **Feel peaceful in decision-making**

- **Feel a greater sense of support in the world**

- **Experience insights about ourselves and others**

- **Enjoy greater peace of mind**

- **Experience fewer regrets as we learn to act from our souls**

Parents who attend my programs often ask me if my philosophies have changed since I started teaching parenting in 1993. The one (and perhaps only) thing I say in my programs today that I didn't say in past years is this: "Listen to your gut! Listen to yourself." Today, I encourage my course participants to follow their instincts, *even* if it means disregarding something they've learned in my course.

Anyone can become more intuitive. Everyone *is* intuitive to a certain extent. Some of us are more practiced at it or consciously intuitive; others are unconsciously intuitive. If you have ever said something like, "I just had a gut feeling . . ." you were listening to your intuition. I have a friend who says she's not intuitive at all, but to me she's "unconsciously intuitive." One day we both showed up an hour early to pick up our children from soccer and found a state of pandemonium. The coach had never arrived and 20 first-graders were running wild. Some scared, some just out of control. After we had restored some peace, I turned to her and asked, "Why are you here so early?" She said, "I don't know, I just had a feeling I should show up early." Without knowing it, she had heeded her intuition.

You've probably had similar experiences:

- **Feeling your child's forehead for no reason and discovering a fever**

- **Knowing what someone is going to say before they say it**

- **Knowing who is calling before you pick up the phone**

We can only nurture and expand our ability to hear our inner guidance once we become consciously aware of it. Catch yourself following your gut. Notice how it feels when your inner voice speaks. Notice what happens when you follow it and what happens when you don't. Over time, you'll hear it more and more clearly.

Developing your intuition is no harder than playing tennis or operating a computer. Like both of these activities, it requires openness to doing things a new way, and lots of practice. If you want to become more intuitive, you can—even if you feel as if you've never experienced any sort of intuitive guidance. The next section will help you develop your intuition and begin to experience the serenity it brings. These practices will help you in business, love relationships, and in every other area of your life.

READY, FIRE, AIM

The prospect of trying this or other new parenting practices may bring up some resistance or skepticism within yourself about the validity of the practice and then about actually following the hunches you get. I urge you to adopt the Ready, Fire, Aim (RFA) approach Thomas Peters described in his bestselling business book *In Search of Excellence*. In other words, try it, then modify as needed. That's how successful companies move ahead and that's how successful parents move ahead as well. If you have any hesitation about any new practice, apply two questions:

1. **Am I certain this practice will not harm my child's self-esteem?**

2. **Might it possibly help our situation?**

If the answer to both questions is "yes," then *Fire*—try the new idea. I've used this process over the years every time I've come across new information. If I feel certain it will not hurt my child, I'll try it. Applying these two questions and the RFA approach saves a lot of time and energy we might invest trying to "figure out" if something will work. Instead of trying to "figure out," if something will work, just do it.

SIX WAYS TO EXPAND YOUR INTUITION

After studying the art of intuition for several years, I've found the following practices to be the most helpful:

Be in Silence Five to 30 Minutes Each Day

In my experience, the single most powerful practice is silence/listening. As the poet Rumi says, "There is a way between voice and presence where information flows. In disciplined silence it opens. With wandering talk it closes." When we sit in silence, we connect to our intuition. When we connect to our intuition, we're much more likely to get the answers that serve our children. Silence is the most direct path to our inner knowing. Sitting in silence helps to quiet the mind. When the mind is quiet, the heart speaks.

My husband's family came to stay with us—13 people in all. For four days, no room was ever quiet. The sounds of family even came through the bathroom doors. I had recently purchased a cell phone and plugged it into an outlet in the kitchen to charge. Unknown to me, I had messages and the phone beeped every two minutes. I did not hear the beep for the entire four days because of the loud talking, TV, and phone ringing incessantly.

It was not until I walked in the door after taking everyone to the airport that I heard the phone beeping. It was completely annoying in the silence to the point that I had to go get the owner's manual and learn how to turn it off. What a powerful reminder: You have to be quiet to hear the message.

Sitting in silence brings peace. When we feel more at peace, the answers we need come to us. Actually, they were always there. Silence allows an avenue for their expression. Do not underestimate the power of this first practice. It's powerful in its simplicity. I'm not saying this is a quick fix for parenting challenges. So often, parents will call me in a crisis desperately wanting a five-minute answer. They do not want to hear about practices and long-term solutions, which is not surprising. We live in a quick-fix society. We've been trained to expect our needs to be met *now*. We can get an overnight package, a drive-through hamburger, and a ten-minute oil change. But there's no quick fix for developing your intuition. You can, however, expect to see small, but immediate changes when you commit to tapping into your inner wisdom through the practice of silence.

Clear the Decks

If you think of intuitive guidance as "being in the flow," it's important to clear anything, visible or invisible, in the way of this flow. Silence clears the distractions of thoughts and sounds. Breathing clears the decks physiologically. Here are some other levels of clearing you might consider:

- **Clear your home and workspace of clutter. Just take a single step. Perhaps it's clearing your desk, bathroom, or kitchen counters at the end of each day.**

- Clear your mind of worry, criticism, and other negative thoughts. When you notice a negative thought, stop mid-way if you can and breathe. Replace it with the most uplifting thought you can come up with. Two of my general-purpose favorites are: *God has something planned for me that's more wonderful than I can imagine.* And *I wonder how this will turn out to be the greatest thing that's ever happened to me.*

- Add some breath to your schedule. If you're busy from the moment you get up until the moment you go to bed, you don't have the time or space to hear your guidance. Eliminate some activities.

- Steer clear of people who sap your energy. Is there anyone in your life who only takes or worries or complains all the time? The more people like this you spend time with, the less likely you'll hear your own voice.

- Clean a cupboard. Everything in our lives reflects everything else in our lives. If we can more easily find something in our physical space, we're more likely to find it in our psychic space.

- Clear the energy by changing activities. If you're feeling bogged down mentally or emotionally, go for a walk or a bike ride. If you've become too isolated, get out of the house and get around people. The change will act like a breath of fresh air. Set the intention of a solution coming to you before you leave, then let it go.

- Clear up any unfinished business. Each bit of incomplete communication, undelivered promises, and unsaid words act like static in our intuitive field. Make it a daily practice to close the loop, make amends, or take care of whatever is hanging out there undone. This gets easier and faster with practice and the rewards are almost immediate.

- Clear anything in the way of love. Intuitive connections are greatly enhanced by being in love with someone, because when you love them, you're deeply in tune with them. If there's anything in the way of love, take care of it. This might mean something as simple as hugging your spouse or touching your child when you haven't done that in the past few hours, or it might mean apologizing.

Inquire Within

Sometimes our intuitive guidance comes to us in a flash. Often, though, we need to invite it to speak. Get into the habit of asking yourself what's going on:

- How am I feeling?

- Do I need a time out?

- How does it make me feel to discipline in this way?

- What is my gut telling me?

- What's the next step I need to take?

After a while, the act of stopping will immediately give you an answer. Notice whether your energy goes up or down when you consider various choices or are around various people. Sometimes we get to the "yes" by noticing the "no's."

Two friends recently went to a French Bistro for a quick dinner on Saturday night. When they got there, they discovered it was closed, so they walked next door to the pizza parlor. After about ten minutes they both agreed that the place didn't feel like where they wanted to eat. They drove a quarter mile to a more upscale café and realized, after sitting down, that this menu wasn't quite what they wanted either. Finally, a local Cajun restaurant came to mind, and off they went. They had an exceptionally fun time, sampling the restaurant's five vegetable dishes. The hostess recognized them from a group they all belonged to and brought them a sample of all three Southern desserts. If both women hadn't been comfortable sharing the "no's" they'd felt in the previous three restaurants, the evening might have turned out much more ordinary.

Children can learn these lessons as well. One day my nine-year-old begged me to go into the local skateboard shop. I didn't want her to because I knew the store carried drug paraphernalia, but since I am a big believer in freedom, we went in. There was angry music blaring and a young man approached us. She looked quickly at some shorts and said, "Okay, let's go." We were back on the street in less than 30 seconds.

I asked, "Why did you leave so quickly?" She said, "That guy had bad energy." I agreed. She asked, "Why did his energy feel so bad?" I said, "I don't know, but it's not so important that we know *why* someone has bad energy. What's most important is that we notice the negative energy and move away from it."

I pointed out that her intuition was speaking to her (she had often said she was not intuitive). I am convinced that she had this helpful experience because she has a peaceful, quiet inner life and I silently stayed in the background and allowed her to have her experience.

Acknowledge Feelings: Yours and Your Child's

Intuition communicates to us through our feelings. Therefore, we must be able to identify, feel, and acknowledge these feelings to clearly hear the messages. Feelings are the expressway to your intuition. As you increase your ability to feel and express them, you'll become more continuously in touch with the rich guidance they offer.

Acknowledge Your Feelings:

Most of us were raised to believe what we were told and not what we felt. "You're fine," "Buck up," "Don't be sad," and other statements intended to soothe us often had the effect of drowning out our intuitive sense. So it's no surprise that most of us don't trust our feelings. Yet it's that trust that helps us feel confident as we parent. In addition, many of us were lied to as children, so it's no wonder we're not certain what our inner guide is telling us. Abraham-Hicks describes children's formative years as "those years when physical man tramples the intuitiveness out of the child."

Teacher and author, Gangaji, says that ineffective ways of dealing with emotions include: run from, fix, act out, and fight it. Most spiritual masters (and therapists) recommend feeling our feelings all the way. If you're not so in touch with your feelings, start by tuning into your body and hearing all the feeling messages from tension to upset to joy. Close your eyes and scan your body from the top of your head to the soles of your feet. What do you notice? Describe both the physical sensations and any emotions. Acknowledging these symptoms helps them move along and clears the way for divine ideas.

If you can't quite figure out what you're feeling emotionally, report your body sensations: "My head feels heavy and I keep getting shivers up and down my back." When I get tense, I make my hands into fists without even knowing it. Only when I take time to check in to my body do I sense this and consciously relax my hands.

In his bestseller, *The Power of Now,* Eckhart Tolle tells us, "Whenever you are waiting, wherever it may be, use that time to feel the inner body. In this way, traffic jams and lines become very enjoyable. Instead of mentally projecting yourself away from the Now, go more deeply into the Now by going more deeply into the body. The art of inner-body awareness will develop into a completely new way of living, a state of permanent connectedness with Being, and will add a depth to your life that you have never known before."

When you can feel your feelings, express them. Write about them. Share them with your spouse or friend. When feelings aren't talked about, the result is anger, aggression and depression. One of my friends keeps a tennis racket under her bed and pounds on it to move her anger through. Another, who's lost several family members and friends, says that the best thing she does is let the grief come when it comes. "Sometimes I don't even know who I'm crying about, but if I let it rip, it passes in about a minute. That's a way different experience than when I believed I should squash all negative feelings down." As she's become more graceful at letting the feelings move through, she's become increasingly intuitive.

Acknowledge Your Child's Feelings:

On a cross-country flight, I sat next to a father of a ten-year-old boy. When he heard that I spoke on the topic of parenting, he started talking about his son. He shared with me that he had just held his son back in fourth grade. "That's a tough one," I said, "How did he take it?" "Oh, I just told him, 'Hey Buddy—better now than later, so get over it!'" Ouch! Being held back a grade is hugely upsetting to any child. Having your feelings discounted makes it even worse.

When we shut down our child's feelings by minimizing, denying, or any number of other emotional stoppers, we sever the communication lines from us to them and from them to their inner guidance. When we acknowledge their feelings, we open the communication lines and teach them a skill critical for hearing their intuition.

In our desire to help our child, we often skip over the important first step of empathizing with how they feel. I don't suggest that you give up processing or giving advice, just acknowledge the feelings first. Ironically, diving into and naming what your child is feeling actually helps them to move through the feeling faster. Rudolf Dreikurs put this aptly when he said, "An emotion that is repressed, persists. Feelings that are accepted or acknowledged lose their destructive charge." What we resist, persists. Soothe first, process later.

Start Small, Start Happy

Don't wait until the heat is on to start tuning in to your intuition. Experiment with tuning in to your inner guidance when you are feeling relaxed and happy. When I drove to Las Vegas with my daughters for a vacation, we played a game Sonia Choquette calls the "I wonder" game. We had been playing this for years, when I discovered this fun name for it in her book *The Wise Child*.

The "I wonder" game is one of the most fun ways to play with and develop your intuition. You simply make guesses about different situations, "I wonder who is on the phone?" "I wonder what time daddy will call us today?" Because of the relaxed nature of the vacation (no schedules, everyone was having fun), our accuracy went through the ceiling.

One day we woke up with a mission to find a car wash for our oversized truck and a place to buy swimsuits for the girls. We pulled out onto the strip and at each light wondered which way to turn. Within ten minutes we located a car wash that could accommodate our large truck and a store that carried children's swimsuits on the same corner!

Start with small, fun situations. Include your kids when you can:

- **Before you look at your watch, guess the time**

- **When you're in a building with several elevators, stand in front of the one you think will come next**

- **Imagine where your parking place will be when you're a block away from a store**

Ask for a Sign . . . or Three

If you're struggling with a decision, ask the universe for three signs. When I was writing this book, I seemed to encounter more obstacles than at any other time of my life, especially when I scheduled writing retreats. My children became ill, huge forest fires broke out, blizzards materialized out of nowhere. One day I was arranging to get out of town for a writing retreat in Mexico and I felt so overwhelmed after dealing with an unfriendly passport agent, I considered giving up the whole book project. I asked for three signs if I was supposed to go ahead.

Almost immediately I realized I could go to the local post office for my passport instead of dealing with the difficult agent in the next town. The man who helped me was not only friendly and kind, clearing all obstacles out of my way, but he called, "Bon Voyage!" as I walked out of the post office. As I drove away, I saw a bald eagle, my special animal that seems to appear as a sign to move forward. Twenty minutes later, as I pulled up at the health foods store, I spotted a car with a bumper sticker I'd designed that said, "Honor Every Student." Three signs in less than an hour.

When you ask for three signs, it's important that you look for them. One friend, who had to decide by midnight if she should move ahead on the purchase of a particular house, wondered if she'd be able to get three signs and agreed to stay alert for them. She was in her home office all day and then teaching a seminar in the evening. She received a fax with her closing costs—$2,000 less than she'd been told. Then, three other signs popped up during her seminar. Your guidance is never limited by your circumstances, only your ability to recognize it.

GOING DEEP
WHEN THE HEAT IS ON

The Dalai Lama says, "If an individual has a calm state of mind, that person's attitudes and views will be calm and tranquil even in the presence of great agitation." A few years ago, my husband and I retuned from a night out to a very upset sitter and three-year-old. While we were gone, my daughter had shoved a small bead far into her ear canal. I called my family doctor and he met us at the local clinic at 9:00 that night. His attempts to remove the bead failed and actually pressed the bead up against the eardrum. He recommended that we go to the hospital emergency room 30 miles away.

I called the hospital and learned that to remove the bead they would need to use general anesthesia. They claimed that they could not risk her moving as they dug out the bead. Additionally, I learned that no pediatrician was on duty that night. When I asked what my other options were, they reluctantly told me that an ear, nose, and throat doctor in a neighboring town was the only doctor who had the extremely high-powered microscope capable of easily extracting the bead and he was not available on a Sunday night. I felt upset and confused.

My husband was frantic and demanded that we take our child to the hospital immediately. I said, "Give me a few minutes of silence," and moved to a quiet room to try and listen to my gut. I emerged within five minutes and announced, "I am not taking our child to the emergency room tonight. I don't want to risk using general anesthesia on a child with no pediatrician on duty." My normally calm husband went ballistic.

"Are you crazy?" he demanded. "Are you going to put our child to bed in pain and with a bead pressed up against her eardrum?"

"Trust me," I said with an eerie calm. My confidence soothed him. I put some olive oil in my child's ear, put her in our bed, and tried in vain to sleep.

I called the ear, nose, and throat specialist first thing the next morning. He agreed to see us right away. When we entered the office, he showed my daughter the big microscope and let her look through it. He and his nurse were comforting. As I took the first of many deep breaths, they placed my child in the "papoose," a friendly word for straightjacket. I held one of her hands and her dad held the other. Within ten seconds the procedure was complete. Out came the bead, followed by giant sighs of relief. No damage to the eardrum, no pain, no general anesthesia, just one sticky bead the nurse put in a special box, and one happy child.

Taking the time to listen to my intuition paid off big. I am not recommending that you not take your child to the emergency room. In fact, on several occasions, we did exactly that. What I am recommending is that you listen to your intuition, in addition to professional advice, about medical care (or anything else). It will take courage at times, but with a few successes under your belt, your confidence (and your ability to hear) will grow.

Once you make the connection to your inner self, you need never again feel insecure or incapable. You will feel more joyful and centered about all of your parenting decisions and that joy will naturally flow over onto other members of your family. Be patient. Intuitive parenting is a day-to-day, minute-to-minute choice. It is the practice of choosing to connect with and listen to your higher self. Then choosing again . . . and again . . . and again. . . . When we choose silence, stillness, and connecting to our intuition, we can truly begin to experience the joy of Parenting with Soul. When we're in touch with our intuition, we can sense when our child is sick before symptoms appear, make more informed choices about how to discipline, and feel better about all of our parenting decisions.

A VISION OF THE FUTURE

Abraham Maslow, psychologist and anthropologist who lived with and studied the Blackfoot Indians in 1938, paints a story from the past that may become our vision of the future:

> [There] was a little boy that I was very fond of. He was about seven or eight years old, and I found by looking very closely that he was a kind of rich kid, in a Blackfoot way. He had several horses and cattle in his name, and he owned a medicine bundle of particular value.
>
> Someone, a grown-up, turned up who wanted to buy the medicine bundle, which was the most valuable thing that he had. I learned from his father that what little Teddy did when he [was] made this offer—remember he was only seven years old—was to go into the wilderness by himself to meditate.
>
> He went away for about two or three days and nights, camping out, thinking for himself. He did not ask his father or mother for advice and they didn't tell him anything. He came back and announced his decision. I can just see us doing that with a seven-year-old kid.

> — *THE RIGHT TO BE HUMAN:*
> *A BIOGRAPHY OF ABRAHAM MASLOW*
> BY EDWARD HOFFMAN

I can see us doing that in some form with a four-year-old, a seven-year-old, or a 16-year-old—if it's been modeled for them by their parents. Tune in and begin today to build their intuitive legacy.

Prayer/Affirmation

I allow myself to hear my inner guidance and joyfully ask and receive the answers that serve me.

Soulful Reminders

- If we learn to hear and follow our inner guidance, we'll dramatically reduce the level of stress in our lives and in our families. We will:
    - ➡ Feel confident about our parenting choices
    - ➡ Feel peaceful in decision-making
    - ➡ Feel a greater sense of support in the world
    - ➡ Experience insights about ourselves and others
    - ➡ Enjoy greater peace of mind
    - ➡ Experience fewer regrets as we learn to act from our souls

- If you have any hesitation about a particular practice, apply two questions:
    - ➡ Am I certain this practice will not harm my child's self-esteem?
    - ➡ Might it possibly help our situation?

- Spending five to 30 minutes a day in silence is the best way to tap your intuition.

- Think of intuitive guidance as "being in the flow." It's important to clear anything, visible or invisible, in the way of this flow.

- Get into the habit of asking yourself what's going on.

- Acknowledge feelings: yours and your child's.

- Tell the truth.

- Start tuning in to your intuition with small, fun situations.

- If you're struggling with a decision, ask the universe for three signs.

THE POWER OF ONE SMALL STEP

Take a moment to affirm your "intuitive" practice for this week. It doesn't have to be something that's difficult or new or gobbles up a lot of time. I started by becoming quiet each time I wanted an answer.

Principle #3
Become
a
Conscious
Creator

11

attract what you want

If you want to parent smarter, not harder, learn how to attract what you want. We threw a birthday bash for our hamster one year and invited a house full of seven-year-old girls and boys. The boys were particularly rambunctious that day and I mentioned to my children that everyone needed to stay inside; no one was allowed to jump on the trampoline. My daughters then walked into the living room where the boys were running wildly. Motioning toward the trampoline, they loudly announced, "Whatever you do today, *do not go on the trampoline!*" A few minutes later I stepped outside to round up the troops and guess what? Three boys were doing back flips on the trampoline. They had gone directly to the place that was pulsing with energy.

My girls had, unwittingly, harnessed the power of a universal principle . . . to work *against* their desires.

If you want to parent with tremendous ease, then master the Law of Attraction, the most powerful universal principle in our lives. Master it, and you will find the answers to all of your parenting challenges.

Anything you want to attract into your life can be yours, and the Law of Attraction holds the key. Once you understand the powerful magnetic effect of your thoughts and feelings, you can work in concert with this law to change your reality.

Stated simply, the Law of Attraction says: "Like attracts like." First written about 2,500 years before Christ—in Buddhist texts—this law holds that "what you think is what you get." The Law of Attraction has shown up in the title of many bestsellers. Norman Vincent Peale called it *The Power of Positive Thinking*. Napoleon Hill coined the phrase *Think and Grow Rich*. Peter McWilliams authored a book titled *You Can't Afford the Luxury of a Negative Thought*.

Our culture acknowledges the Law of Attraction with colloquialisms like, "birds of a feather flock together," "misery loves company," and "the apple doesn't fall far from the tree." I'm here to challenge this last assertion. I fully expect that, as we parents master the Law of Attraction and other spiritual principles in this book, the next generation can become remarkably different parents.

In a fresh interpretation of the Law of Attraction, Neale Donald Walsch, author of *Conversations with God*, likens the universe to a big copy machine that grants our every vibration and thought. If this is true—if what we think is what we get—then why don't we get what we *say* we want? Why do our affirmations fail? And how do we begin to attract into our life what we want? The answer is: by bringing congruence to our thoughts and words, and becoming a conscious creator.

BECOME A CONSCIOUS CREATOR

We use amplifiers, either consciously or unconsciously. You amplify something by talking about it, thinking about it, feeling it, discussing it, or picturing the details. You can direct your thoughts and energy to create whatever you want. This is not as strange as it may seem. You already do this everyday, perhaps without conscious awareness. The formula for manifestation is simple and we can use it with every problem in parenting. To apply The Law of Attraction most powerfully, memorize this recipe:

Strong Feelings + Repetition = Manifestation

Apply this recipe to each of the steps I'll share with you later in this chapter. Notice that the formula does not say Strong *positive* feelings + Repetition = Manifestation. In other words, you can manifest something negative—something you don't want (like children jumping on the trampoline)—if you repeatedly feel your negative feelings about it. We often create by default. Instead, ask, "What do I want more of?" because this combines positive feelings with repetition and moves you toward your heart's desires. You're getting what you think about whether you know it or not. Thoughts without emotion have lower creative power. Emotion is like fuel.

The Seven Steps in Creation/Manifestation Are:

1. **Notice: what you don't have, a problem, a challenge (contrast)**

2. **Acknowledge what you want**

3. **Flow energy toward it; vibrate with it**

4. **Attract it to you**

5. **Allow it in**

6. **Become big enough to sustain it**

7. **Take it for "granted"**

As you review these steps, notice where you get hung up. Some of us stay at step one most of our lives, complaining about what we don't have, instead of using that as a launching pad to manifest what we want. Some of us get stuck at step two because we don't know what we want. The idea of flowing energy and vibrating with the idea of what we want in step three may feel too "out there" for some people. Others can attract good things but then have trouble allowing them in.

Have you ever felt overwhelmed by a gift or deflected a compliment? If so, you're not allowing it in. After many months of searching, Phil and Mary magically manifested a wonderful house with a pool on half an acre in a prestigious community called Atherton in the San Francisco Bay Area. The owner took a second mortgage and both brokers reduced their commissions, and within weeks they were living in the house of their dreams. They noticed that for about six months they mumbled the name of their community whenever people asked where they lived, feeling as if on some level they didn't deserve it. And for several weeks after they moved in, Mary half expected someone to come to the door and say, "Get out!" No one did, and eventually they grew into their home.

FOCUS ON WHAT YOU WANT

I was working out in one of those huge 24-hour fitness centers one day and I looked up to see a long row of televisions across the wall, each tuned to a different channel. I don't watch TV, but it was impossible to avoid these since I was working out on a machine right in front of them. My brain and eyes wanted to take in all the different screens, especially since I was not wearing the TV headphones. Finally, to keep myself from going bonkers, I focused in on only one TV. It was difficult at first to maintain the concentration, but it was a powerful exercise in developing a laser focus. In life, it's important that we focus only on the "television" that pictures what we want more of.

As we come to understand the Law of Attraction, we realize that what we think is what we get. So it becomes imperative to hold *good* thoughts if we want to attract *good* into our lives. Many of us think we have no control of how we feel. We think that conditions have to change before we feel good. Buddha declared, "We are what we think. All that we are arises with our thoughts. With our thoughts, we make the world." I suggest you find any excuse to feel good, instead of just waiting for the conditions to change. In fact, you don't even need an excuse. Abraham-Hicks tells us, "You cannot monitor your thoughts. Monitor how you feel. If you feel bad, you are probably thinking about something that is misaligned. See yourself as you are wanting to be, and from that place you will attract more of that." Decide to feel good and watch what happens. If you need a boost, move your body, breathe, or change activities. I often feel amazed at the impact these simple actions can have on my mood.

Some people come to the mistaken conclusion, "I can't be happy unless my current parenting challenges change and I can't change them, so I guess I'll just be unhappy." Instead, allow your current parenting challenges to produce a new desire, and then you can train yourself to feel good in lots of different situations. For example, if you have a child who wakes up several times each night with bad dreams, instead of focusing on your interrupted sleep, substitute the desire to be the best parent you can be or the desire to awaken rested and refreshed. If your child is coming home with poor grades, focus on your desire that your child feel happy and fulfilled, no matter what his educational or work path may be.

The best remedy for a negative thought is a positive thought. When you feel negative, get into the habit of asking yourself, "What do I *want* in this situation?" This will help you focus on the good feelings associated with what you want instead of the bad feelings you associate with the current challenge.

A grandmother called me distraught because her grandchild had been hit and verbally abused by her custodial parent. "Every time I think about it, I feel so terrible," she said. "What would happen if you chose not to think about it," I asked. This may sound like harsh advice at first, but in reality, does feeling bad accomplish anything? The grandmother had taken steps to get help for the family. There was nothing more she could do, except pray for them, change her focus, and remember that many great people have come from difficult home situations. She told me later that this had been a turning point for her, that it gave her permission to stop fretting and worrying, and helped unhook a generations-long unhealthy dynamic in her family.

As you might imagine, hearing of child abuse touches me deeply, and this is the technique I use when I see or hear of children who are being mistreated. I silently bless the child and parent, and hold a picture of the highest possible outcome. I know a good outcome is possible because it happened to me. The verbal abuse I experienced as a child motivated me to find a better way as a parent and to help other parents do the same. This book is one of the results. My peaceful family is the other.

Focus on the current reality only if it's exactly what you want, or only long enough to define the problem and do the next right thing.

Warning! You will find little support out there for this practice. You may be tempted to commiserate with friends and relatives. Misery does love company, but happiness loves company, too. When you decide to be happy and positive, you will likely attract more people in your life who are positive thinkers and you may leave behind those who are not ready to give up old habits of negative thinking. What a joy to be surrounded with people who are willing and able to support you on your journey to positive parenting. The next suggestion zeroes in a bit more on the way to focus.

VISUALIZE A POSITIVE OUTCOME

Fast forward seeing things as you would like them to be as if they already are. From that point of being, you will attract more. Make it real and it will become real. When we picture what we want, we help bring it into being. Visualization has become a popular buzzword, and it's likely you're already somewhat familiar with the technique. No doubt you know this means picturing in your mind a positive result (children sleeping through the night; a family vacation that's filled with harmony and joy; peaceful mealtimes during which everyone gets the appropriate nutrition). Let me add a layer or two to this practice.

First, take a deep breath. Then picture the outcome and experience the feelings you expect to have when this happens. If possible, use all your senses: How will it look, taste, feel, smell, sound? Does it seem in alignment with your goals and values? Is this for the best and highest reasons? If possible, use some symbols in your environment to represent this picture. For the harmonious family vacation, you might have brochures from the destination or a happy photo of your family on another vacation.

My first exposure to visualization happened in 1976 when my whole family was glued to the TV set watching the summer Olympics in Montreal. One of the highlights was watching American Bruce Jenner capture the gold medal in the decathlon. Not only did he have the highest overall point total to land the gold, he also won *each and every one* of the decathlon events.

Bruce later shared how he mentally prepared for this awesome feat: On the ceiling above his bed, he had taped pictures of himself winning every decathlon event. These images were the first thing he woke up to each morning and the last thing in his mind each night. It was these images, he said, that inspired him to train for and ultimately win the decathlon.

I grabbed hold of this idea of visualizing what I wanted, but felt unsure about how it all worked. (I did, however, start eating Wheaties after his picture appeared on the box.) I began visualizing and noticed I would not always get what I had visualized. After learning more about the Law of Attraction, I realized that in the course of visualizing what I wanted, I was directing *more* attention to the *distance* between me and what I wanted than I was to what I actually wanted. Of course, I was getting exactly what I had visualized—the distance. As Deepak Chopra said, "If you project the same images everyday, your reality will be the same everyday." When I learned to focus on the outcome, *not* the distance from here to there, I manifested that outcome.

Here's another example: I have a child who has never been very interested in eating. She is thin and she is the one the grandmas are always telling to eat. I felt upset every time I prepared a meal and she objected and asked for cereal. So I started visualizing. I pictured a calm and centered mealtime and a healthy child. I let go and set out a variety of different foods. My daughter is still thin and, when I remembered that I was that thin as a child, I let go even more. We enjoy calm and centered mealtimes, and she has enjoyed radiant health most of her life. Observe less. Visualize more. Take your mind off whatever negativity may be happening right now.

PRACTICE THE 90/10 RULE

The Old Testament tells us, "As [a man] thinketh in his heart so is he," and the New Testament agrees: "According to your faith it is done unto you." The 90/10 Rule describes a measurable way to redirect your attention from the *problems* to the *possibilities*. The practice of 90/10 *attracts* better behavior from your children and a more positive and uplifting experience for you as a parent.

I think few of us would describe parenting as easy. Everyday presents new challenges, and we all need to vent sometimes. Venting can help us move through our negative emotions and back into a peaceful place. Native Americans and other indigenous cultures understand this and incorporate regular ceremonies in which specific dancers embody the built-up anger and frustration of the tribe, who shout their support from the sidelines. I have even heard of one family that had a special room designated where kids could yell, scream, and throw things when they felt the need. I like to do a hard workout when I'm angry and upset. It seems to help the emotion pass through quickly and converts it into energy. In general, though, our culture doesn't offer many healthy ways to vent. Instead, it leaks out in road rage or by indulging in what seem to be the most pervasive national pastimes—negativity, cynicism, and complaining.

As parents, we often find that what attracts our attention and what we focus on are parenting "problems." How much time did you spend during the past 24 hours focusing on your child's problems? For years I found myself focusing on the fights, the misbehavior, and the negative things my children did. Society, my friends, and my family often supported me in this practice. Focusing on the "problem," researching the "problem," and working on the "problem" made me a "good mother." Through these actions, I was demonstrating my genuine concern for my children. The Law of Attraction says my focus on problems was only *increasing* the problems. In retrospect, I see the truth in this.

Inspiration for the 90/10 practice came from a phone call several years ago with my friend Tyler a fellow traveler on the conscious parenting path. I felt so upset about how Brianna, then five, had been treating her two-year-old sister Alexa. The sibling rivalry had been intense in the previous weeks and Brianna had been particularly mean to her sister that day. She had jerked toys away from her, pushed her down, called her names, and left Alexa crying on the floor.

I felt so upset. It really hurt to watch one of my children deliberately harm the other! And it wasn't the first time. Had I done something wrong? Was I not setting a good example? What could I do to stop this? I was close to tears, and called Tyler out of sheer frustration.

As we talked, she acknowledged my feelings and listened, and I started to feel a little better. After hearing me out, she then shared her list of complaints about her son. Both of us felt relieved that we weren't alone, and venting helped. After hanging up I noticed I felt bad. A little voice inside was saying something to me. Without knowing exactly why, I called Tyler back. She was feeling bad, too! Our conversation had discouraged both of us. Tyler and I knew about the power of the Law of Attraction— we had just temporarily forgotten. We realized "what you focus on grows," so we wanted a practice that was aligned with that truth.

We knew it was somewhat helpful to vent. We knew it was even more important to focus on *what we want*. So we agreed to spend *ten percent* of our time and energy venting and defining the problem and *90 percent* of our time focusing on what we want. The ten percent gave us the opportunity to be heard and to get clear about the problem, and we used the bulk of our time and energy, the 90 percent, to harness the Law of Attraction.

We began to change our lives that day. We felt uncomfortable and clumsy at first, but we were committed to focusing on what we wanted. We both wanted a loving home. We wanted to raise children who treat one another with kindness. Most of all, we wanted to feel peaceful and happy in the presence of our children.

In my home, I started to send more energy and attention to the behaviors that I wanted. For starters, when I noticed Brianna treating her sister nicely, I said (through gritted teeth, at first), "You are so kind and thoughtful." In the beginning, my thoughts and words were not aligned. I said the "right" words, while my mind raced with thoughts like, "But you were mean 28 other times today!" Over the next few months, my words and my beliefs slowly began to align and I moved up the vibration scale closer to my desired state. Then one day, I noticed that my thoughts and my words were completely congruent. I watched for times when Brianna treated her sister nicely. "Brianna is thoughtful, helpful, and kind," I would to say to my friends and her father—often in earshot of Brianna. I was sincere. I meant every word to my core.

Another example is when the kids are cleaning up their toys in the den, but they walk away before it's done, avoid focusing on what you don't want: "Hey you guys—get back here. You're not even done!" Focus on what you want: "Great job! Just a few more things to pick up."

REFUSE TO REGURGITATE
THE NEGATIVE

Would you attempt to drive your car by looking out the back window? Of course not. But we do something similar as parents when we dredge up the past in an effort to improve a situation. Almost all negativity requires that you reference the past, and when we're hanging back in the past, we're not moving forward to create the lives we want. Make it your motto to never complain and never explain. When you make a mistake, instead of over-apologizing (which some people do instead of changing their behavior), acknowledge your mistake, learn, and let your future behavior be a living amends. One of my amends sounded like this, "I was late picking you up. I made a mistake, and I feel bad that I upset you.

I'll do my best to always be on time." And I haven't done that since.

A classic case of regurgitating the negative often happens when a mom, pregnant with her first child, begins to ask other women about their labor and deliveries. I was astounded at how many mothers were so willing to horrify me with their stories of never-ending labors. Take this special opportunity to help that mother-to-be set the tone and focus on the experience she wants.

When you make a commitment to stay out of the negative and out of the past, you may be surprised at how hard it is at first to have a conversation, because most of our conversations are about the past. What, then, can you talk about? Anything that's true in the present moment: Your feelings, hopes, and dreams. One of the 14 precepts of Buddhism says to avoid discussing anyone who is not present. Add that to your conversational mix, and you'll find there is more silence, more space, and an environment for the essence of each person to be present, free of the drag of negativity and the past.

On one of my many days at home alone with the kids, I invited two of their friends over. Over the course of the day, they dropped glasses twice on the tile floor and each time I had to vacuum and mop the kitchen. I had suggested that the other children come over because usually my children seemed happy and content playing with their friends all day and got a break from one another. This day, however, the kids fought most of the time. I mediated fight after fight and felt burned out by lunchtime. In the afternoon, they went outside to play (after more fighting), forgot to take their boots off when they came in, and left gobs of mud on the kitchen floor (which, as you may recall, I had cleaned twice). I love my children's friends, but I had never been so happy to see them go.

A few moments later, my husband, Joe, walked in and asked, "How was your day?"

Before I go on, let me tell you a little about my husband's job. His "office" is the pristine slopes of the world-class resort: Aspen. His day consists of skiing in the powder and sunshine and being wined and dined in some of the country's finest restaurants. He is a professional ski instructor for an international mix of top CEOs, real estate moguls, and super models.

He walks in tanned and relaxed and asks, "How was your day?"

At that point, I have a choice. I can resurrect the horrors of my day and experience more negativity, or—knowing that I attract with every thought, word, and action—I can answer (with gusto), "I feel great!"

I don't always succeed at refusing to regurgitate the negative, but I'm getting better and better at it and can testify that succeeding at this increases the quality of life for everyone. I'm not asking you to become Pollyanna or to deny or bury your feelings. If you feel upset, express it and then do what you need to do to move up the vibration scale.

The 90/10 Rule paid off big time. It didn't happen overnight—I sometimes relapsed into focusing on the negative. But slowly my attention has shifted from the problem (Brianna being mean to her sister) to what I wanted (Brianna treating her sister kindly). And today, seven years later, my children love and adore one another. They often work out their fights using peaceful conflict resolution. Just this morning, I could hardly get them up in time for school because they were locked in a full-body hug for over 15 minutes! Harmony is the prevailing condition of our home. It's not *always* peaceful, of course. Negativity still breaks out, but it no longer resembles the epidemic it had been.

Next time you face a parenting challenge, notice where you send most of your energy: to the problem, or to the possibilities? As strange and unnatural as it may feel at first, practice sending more energy to the solution—to *what you want*. Talk about what you want. Think about what you want. Imagine what you want. Flow energy and attention to what you want. And bask in joy as you harvest the rewards. A special note: Lectures almost always violate the 90/10 Rule and are typically a 10/90 experience for everyone.

FOCUS ON THE ESSENCE, NOT THE SPECIFICS, OF WHAT YOU WANT

I ran into a woman I hadn't seen for several years and noticed she was pregnant. I asked the standard question, "Do you know what you're having?" "Oh, yes," she said with utmost certainty, "I am having a grand piano player." I laughed. She stiffened slightly and said, "I'm not kidding. This child is going to be a world-famous grand piano player!" This woman was serious! I congratulated her and moved on feeling a pang of sadness for the unborn child, who may prefer mathematics to Mozart.

We can limit our good and even get into trouble when we get too specific in our desires (verbally or nonverbally). When we delineate the particulars, we may become attached to an outcome and our child, sensing that, may become resistant. Also, when we get too specific, we may limit our good. The parent who holds the specific picture of a child going to college might want to replace that with the picture of a child who's passionate about learning and makes a contribution to the world though her work. Essence is a *quality,* not confined to a specific expression. We can all think of situations where the ultimate outcome was far better than we had imagined, like the highschool dropout who later discovered the theory of relativity. We need to loosen our grip and generalize our intentions to unleash the magic of universal laws, which are here to serve us, if only we know how to work with them. A good all-purpose focus is the desire most parents have: a child who feels happy. Play with this idea today and watch what happens.

One practical way we can become less specific on a daily basis is to ask our children to problem-solve instead of issuing orders at them. Instead of saying, "You *will* be dressed by 7:30 so we can be on time in the morning," substitute this: "How can we get out the door in the morning and have everyone be in a good mood?" Focus on the essence of what you want and allow the universe to deliver that which is best suited for you. When we get too specific, we prevent the power of the universe to provide a solution that's most in harmony with our core desires.

When you're helping your child create what he wants, have him focus on the *why* and the *what* (general) of what he wants, not the *how* (specific).

PUTTING IT ALL TOGETHER

We attract what we are. As Dr. Wayne Dyer says, "You become what you think about each day and those days become your lifetime." Use the Law of Attraction to create the parenting experience and become the parent you've always wanted to be. Or in the Buddha's words:

> The thought manifests as the word;
> The word manifests as the deed;
> The deed develops into habit;
> And habit hardens into character.
> So watch the thought and its ways with care,
> And let it spring from love
> Born out of concern for all beings.
> As the shadow follows the body.
> As we think, so we become.

Prayer/Affirmation

I am a powerful creator,
and I work in harmony with universal principles
to create more harmony in my home.

Soulful Reminders

- **We can become either conscious creators or creators by default.**

- **The seven steps in creation/manifestation are:**
    - ➡ **Notice: what you don't have, a problem, a challenge (contrast)**

➠ Acknowledge what you want

➠ Flow energy toward it; vibrate with it

➠ Attract it to you

➠ Allow it in

➠ Become big enough to sustain it

➠ Take it for "granted"

- Focus on what makes you feel good.

- Follow the 90/10 Rule; 90 percent of our words should be positive and uplifting.

- Focus on the essence, not the specifics, of what you want.

- Visualize a positive outcome.

- Refuse to regurgitate the past.

- Practice joyous anticipation.

The Power of One Small Step

Write down one practice you learned or were reminded of in this chapter that you will use this week to attract the parenting experience you want. I started by thinking more about what I wanted and less about what I did not want.

Principle #4
Live
in
Integrity

12

parent on higher ground

Nearly every parent who completes the Fast Forward exercise in Chapter Two envisions raising an honest child who keeps agreements. Yet, how many of us model this on a consistent basis? You'll parent on higher ground if you adopt integrity as one of your core values.

When I was about ten years old, I sat down to eat dinner to some sort of mystery meat and asked my parents, "What is this?" "Venison," they replied. It smelled funny, but I had enjoyed venison in the past so I ate it. The next day I was in the kitchen when I spotted a container that read "liver" on top of the pile of kitchen trash. "Liver, that's sooooo gross!" I exclaimed. "Oh really?" said my parents smugly, "You seemed to enjoy it last night when you *ate it for dinner.*" I felt humiliated and devastated. I felt profoundly manipulated, betrayed and embarrassed at my ignorance. I distinctly remember deciding at that moment that I could not trust my parents.

That day I personally experienced the beginning of the downward spiral that Gay Hendricks described when he said, "Nearly every personal or corporate disaster begins with an integrity problem and often a small problem." If you want your children to feel close to you when they're teenagers, commit right now to live in integrity. If you want to model personal courage and congruence to your children, live in integrity. If you want long-term harmony and closeness, live in integrity. If you want to free up creative energy, live in integrity.

The Latin roots of the word *integrity* mean "entire." When we live in integrity, we become whole persons. Integrity is to our lives as coal is to a train engine. The power that results when we vibrate in integrity reverberates through our thoughts, words, and actions, affecting our children and generations to come. To parent on higher ground and reap the benefits of living in integrity, follow Hendricks' definition: *speak your truth at all times, share your genuine feelings, and align your thoughts, words, and actions.* Neale Donald Walsh calls this "being transparent." When we are willing to be, as he says, "as transparent as a window pane," our relationships thrive and the universe lines up to support us.

It may not feel like a gratifying experience initially. When you commit to live in integrity, tell the truth, communicate your feelings, and keep your commitments, you may experience short-term disruptions in your family. It may seem easier in the moment to tell a little white lie ("No, sweetie, you can't play with Shannon today. I called, and no one was home.") than it is to speak the whole truth ("I prefer that you stay home today."). That's a small price to pay for the huge amounts of mental energy you'll free up and the long-term richness you'll create in your relationship with your child.

When we model integrity, we empower our children to develop a healthy conscience that will serve as their inner guide. When you make a mistake, share the truth of who you are, despite any feelings of vulnerability. You'll be showing your children how to step back into integrity when they slip as well. Let's explore the three aspects of this core quality at greater depth.

SPEAK YOUR TRUTH
AT ALL TIMES

Sometimes we lie to protect our children, and sometimes we lie to control. Every time we lie, even if it's for the best of intentions, we break our connection with our child and with our Self. Lying seeps energy from us as we attempt to manage the gap between what is and our version of what is—energy that could be used to enjoy our families and enjoy life. Even if our children don't catch us in the lie, they sense the disconnect.

Withholding information and telling partial truths are also forms of lying. If you get violently angry because your child lied to you, it's a good time to ask yourself if you've been lying to your child, or otherwise. Make the decision right now to end any legacy of lying with you.

Sheila, one of my students, who does her best to always tell the truth, was hiking with her children when they saw a coyote carrying some prey (a house cat) across a field. "Is that a cat in his mouth?" her sensitive nine-year-old son asked. Wanting to soften her son's upset, she answered that it looked like some kind of wild rabbit. "With a rhinestone collar?" the child replied.

We're either lying or telling the truth. There are no shades of gray if we want to stay connected to integrity and to our children. Sheila immediately took three deep breaths, acknowledged that her son was correct, and told him how sad she felt that someone's pet had died. Her son felt connected by her truth, felt his sadness as well, then continued on with their walk.

A teenager who attended one of my workshops shared a common complaint about her parents' breaches of integrity. She and her sister had gone shopping with her dad one day. He spotted a fishing boat that he wanted, now on sale for $2,500. He put the boat on layaway with $800 down and told the girls that he would buy them each a new outfit if they told their mom that $800 was the full price of the boat. She was angry about her parents telling them to be honest yet asking them to lie.

Whether we tell a big lie or just ask our children to tell a caller we are not home right now, our children are watching closely and learning from our *actions,* not what we say. The consequences of being out of integrity are that our children learn by observing our behavior that small (or big) lies are acceptable. They feel hurt when they are harshly held accountable for something their parents get away with, and this may ultimately erode their trust and respect. Also, in the words of Jonathan Cainer, "When we are deliberately dishonest, we harm our own ability to think clearly. We also cause confusion in the minds of others. We prevent them from being able to trust their instincts."

Speak your truth in a loving way at all times. Ironically, if you feel stumped by a situation, tell your child, "I don't know what to say," while feeling your confusion. You then create connection because you're fully present and speaking authentically. This can be especially effective with teenagers.

As a guide to the truth, ask yourself these two key questions:

Am I Being Authentic with Myself?

Are there any places in my life where I am lying to myself? Am I avoiding facing reality in some way? What am I not seeing? If you're feeling particularly courageous, you might ask three close friends or relatives what they see about you that you don't seem to see. Look for any patterns in their responses.

Are There Any Distortions in My Communications?

Do you make threats you don't mean? Empty threats cause our children to not trust us. Do your nos mean "no"? In one of my classes we were discussing the phenomenon of parents who say "no" then give in to their child. One father commented, "I wonder if that's how men first learn that "no" doesn't mean "no." The class was silent as this realization settled in. Children learn what we model.

SHARE YOUR GENUINE FEELINGS

There's something magical about sharing your true feelings. It clears away any obstacles to connection to your child and to your inner guidance.

Many parents attempt to shelter their children from their personal ups and downs; others share too much, dumping their personal stuff on their kids or looking to their children as confidants. Find the middle—that's where integrity lives. Children are highly sensitive and know when something's off. If I'm driving in the car after a rough day at work, our dialogue might look like this:

Out of Integrity:

"Mommy, what's wrong?"

"Nothing." (When it's not true)

Dumping:

"Mommy, what's wrong?"

"I had a really bad day at work. I am so mad. My employees did not show up on time for the big party I was catering. Do you know what else they did? They. . ."

Living in Integrity by Sharing Our True Feelings:

"Mommy, what's wrong?"

"I've had kind of a rough day at work. I do feel a little sad about that."

Your feelings are a key part of the integrity equation. You must be able to identify and name the three biggies: anger, fear, and sadness. We get out of integrity with ourselves when we don't know how we are feeling. When we refuse to share our true feelings with our children or—at the other extreme—dump on them, we disconnect from them.

ALIGN YOUR THOUGHTS, WORDS, AND ACTIONS

Do you do what you say you'll do? Keep the small agreements as well as the big ones. We love our kids and sometimes, to foster a connection with them in the moment, we over-promise. This happens whenever we allow the joy our child feels at the moment we make the promise to become more important than *keeping* the promise. When we make our gratification more important than theirs, it's a setup for disappointment. Eventually, they will stop trusting us.

Over-promising is an aspect of the "adrenaline lifestyle" many of us live. When we over-promise, we can actually cause a rush of adrenaline, on which many of us are hooked. That's the most common reason we do it. Other reasons include:

- **We genuinely want our children to be happy**

- **It's hard to say "no"**

- **To get them off our backs temporarily**

- **To fulfill a selfish need to "look good" in the moment**

Resist the urge to over-promise. In fact, if you tend to over-promise, deliberately make a habit of under-promising during this next week. As a recovering adrenaline addict, I understand the magnitude of this request. Understanding the change process will help you. Remember: To change, you must first gain information and then—and this is important—you must notice and lovingly *accept* yourself when you fall short of your goals. For me, this meant a lot of self-talk like, "Oops, I did it again. I over-promised. How about that? Wasn't that interesting?" Slowly, small successes came. I was increasingly able to stop myself during the adrenaline rush of making a promise that I was not likely to fulfill.

During the time that I was intensely practicing under-promising, my daughter Brianna saw a note that said, "Under-Promise" on the bulletin board in my office. "What does that mean?" she asked. "You know how I said I couldn't pick you up after school last week, that you'd have to ride the bus home, then I showed up at school to give you a ride home and surprised you? Would you rather have me over-promise and say I'll be there, then have to call your teachers to tell you to ride the bus if I can't make it?" "Oh, definitely under-promise," she said emphatically. Once you start under-promising, *you will* discover as I have, that the incredible joy your child feels when you over-deliver far outweighs the short-term rush you feel when you make an empty promise.

On my continuing journey to the realm of under-promising, I am blessed to have a remarkable teacher—my husband. Joe has mastered under-promising and over-delivering. It's one of the many attributes that strongly connects him with his children, his business associates, his friends, and his wife! One of Joe's unspoken "rules" for communicating is that he does not even say "maybe" if there is any chance of dashing someone's hopes.

On one of the occasions that my older daughter made the honor roll, she asked if I could attend the awards assembly. I explained that I would be out of town. She then turned to her father and asked, "Dad, can you come? I really, really want someone to watch me get my certificate." "I can't make it," he said, "there's too much going on at work." I felt disappointed. I had always attended the awards assembly and knew what it meant to her to have me there. I also knew there was a possibility that Joe could make the assembly and could feel the moment when I desperately wanted him to soothe Brianna by saying, "Maybe I can make it." I could almost taste it. *That's* the adrenaline rush. That's the moment to recognize and resist getting a quick hit now at the risk of our child's disappointment later.

I arranged for a friend of mine, who is close to Brianna, to attend the assembly, and Brianna felt quite happy with this plan. When I returned home, I called my friend to see if she got there okay and how it went. "Did you make it to the assembly?" I asked. Through tears she said, "Yes, I did and guess who else was there? Joe. Your husband drove an hour, round-trip, to attend a ten-minute awards ceremony. And you should have seen your daughter's eyes light up when she saw him in the audience."

INTEGRITY IN ACTION: FACING YOUR MISTAKES

We all get out of integrity. The job is to get back in as quickly as you notice, whether it's a day, a minute, or a few hours later. One of the best ways to do this is the F.A.C.T. approach developed by Gay Hendricks. I discovered this model several years ago and began to apply it to all of my relationships. It was not easy to practice this at first (and still often feels challenging), though I'm certain that I owe my deep connection to my husband and children to this process. Gay graciously agreed to allow me to share this process with you. If you use this approach preventively, you can smooth out situations in ten minutes that might take months to handle otherwise. The steps in the process are:

- **Face**

- **Accept**

- **Choose**

- **Take Action**

Step One: Face

Buddha said, "All human unhappiness comes from not facing reality squarely, exactly as it is." Face the unvarnished truth of what you've done. Face it fully and with courage. Face it in detail.

- **What's the reality of the situation?**

- **How am I, or others, out of integrity?**

- **How do I want it to be?**

- **Have I communicated anything untrue to myself or to anybody else in the whole course of this situation?**

- **Have I broken any agreements in the course of this situation? With myself or with others?**

- **If untruths or broken agreements have come to light, the action step(s) I will take to rectify them is (are) _____ and I'll do it (them) by _____.**

Step Two: Accept

Once you have faced the issue squarely, you are ready for acceptance. Complete acceptance of a situation, exactly as it is, creates an openness to change.

- **What about this situation have I not accepted exactly as it is?**

- **Is it something about myself?**

- **Is it something about someone else?**

- **Is it something in the past?**

- **Is it something that's happening now?**

Take a moment now to accept it, just as it is. (Breathing helps.)

Step Three: Choose

Once you have faced and accepted a situation thoroughly, you are in a clear position from which to choose how you would like things to be.

- **What do you most want in this situation?**

Step Four: Take Action

Once you have faced, accepted, and chosen, the next step is to design the required actions.

- **What action(s) can you take to support your getting what you most want in this situation?**

- **I commit to taking the action(s) by _____.**

When you own up to a missed agreement, do your best to avoid blame, excuses, or promising to do better. Keep it straightforward and simple: "Honey, I said I would buy some new markers today, and I didn't do it." When you catch yourself telling less than the whole truth to your child, set it straight in ten seconds by saying, "You know, I didn't tell you the whole truth. I didn't tell you that . . ."

F.A.C.T. IN ACTION

On the way to an outdoor concert with another family, we passed an ice cream store and all six kids (ages three to 13) screamed for ice cream. We wanted to get to the concert, so the adults promised we could stop for ice cream on the way back (our first mistake—over-promising). On the way home, the three youngest children were sleeping and the adults were exhausted from hauling gear and sitting in a huge traffic jam. When one of the children reminded us of the ice cream promise, one of the other moms said, "The store is closed. We'll go tomorrow." We then took the back way home to avoid passing the *open* ice cream store. Here is how I used F.A.C.T. to get back in integrity with my children. I did not meddle with the other parents and their children:

Step One: Face

How am I, or others, out of integrity? The other parent was out of integrity because she lied about the store being open. I was out of integrity because I did not tell my children the truth. I remained silent. **How do I want it to be?** I sensed that the older children were not buying the lie and felt bad. I want to model honesty, have the courage to face the children's upset over the broken agreement, and, after acknowledging their disappointment, make a new agreement. *Have I broken any agreements in the course of this situation?* Yes, the agreement to take them for ice cream. *With myself or with others?* With others.

If untruths or broken agreements have come to light, the action step(s) I will take to rectify them is: to tell my children the truth and reschedule the ice cream outing. **And** *I'll do it (them) by:* when I get home.

Step Two: Accept

Once you have faced the issue squarely, you are ready for acceptance. Complete acceptance of a situation, exactly as it is, creates an openness to change.

What about this situation have I not accepted, exactly as it is? I was judging the parent who lied. *Is it something about myself?* I felt bad about not speaking the truth. I then took a moment to accept the situation just as it was. And I breathed for a few minutes as I took that in.

Step Three: Choose

Once you have faced and accepted a situation thoroughly, you are in a clear position from which to choose how you would like things to be.

What do you most want in this situation? A clear conscience, to model honesty to my children, and the connection that comes with that.

Step Four: Take Action

Once you have faced, accepted, and chosen, the next step is to design the required actions.

What action(s) can you take to support your getting what you most want in this situation? I told my children the truth as soon as we got home and apologized for not speaking up when they were lied to. We agreed that since the little ones were sleeping we would send someone to the store for ice cream sundae ingredients and have ice cream at home.

PARENTING ON HIGHER GROUND WHILE KEEPING THE MAGIC ALIVE

My five-year-old came to me one Christmas asking if Santa was real. (It seems that her older sister had exposed the "sham.") I told her that every child who asks this question is ready to hear the true story of Santa Claus. I then explained that she would indeed get to hear the "Santa Story" that night at bedtime. This gave me time to clear anything that would get in the way of speaking my truth. Additionally, her anticipation and excitement built up throughout the day, footnoting underscoring the importance of the story.

As the girls settled in for their nightly story, I noticed that I felt excited for the chance to speak my truth to my five-year-old and grateful for the opportunity to set the record straight with my eight-year-old. (It's never too late to speak your truth!)

I then spoke *my* deepest truth: "Long ago, in a tiny village, lived a very generous man—the town toy maker. He and his wife loved children very much, but were not able to have any of their own. So one year at Christmastime, they made toys for all the children of the village and carefully placed them in their homes while they were sleeping.

"The children were overjoyed as they woke to find toys made especially for them. This is the legend of Mr. and Mrs. Santa Claus. Since Mr. and Mrs. Claus could not possibly make or buy toys for every child in the world, the parents of all children who celebrate Christmas are entrusted to keep the magic and spirit of Santa Claus alive.

"Parents keep the spirit alive by choosing toys for their children and placing them under the tree each Christmas morning. This is a very special part of being a parent. Then, whenever a child asks if Santa is real, this is a sign to the parent that the child is ready to hear the true meaning of Santa Claus. If you decide to become a parent, you too will get to keep the magic of Santa alive for your children. That way, the legend of Santa, who was so loving and giving, can live on forever."

As I finished the story, I was overcome with the joy and peace I feel when I speak my truth. I had created a rich tradition for my youngest daughter and restored faith in my eldest.

The sweet expressions on my children's faces as they drifted off into slumber confirmed that night that there is something even more wonderful than the magic of Christmas—the power of integrity and magic merged.

Prayer/Affirmation

When I speak my truth at all times,
acknowledge my feelings,
and align my thoughts, words, and actions,
I become a whole parent.

Soulful Reminders

- We must live the qualities we want to see in our children.

- Speak your truth at all times.

- Acknowledge your genuine feelings.

- Align your thoughts, words, and actions.

- We all get out of integrity. The job is to get back in as quickly as you can.

- When you make a mistake:
  - Face the reality of the situation
  - Accept yourself despite the lapse
  - Choose how you want it to be
  - Take a specific action by a specific date

- It's possible to both parent on higher ground and keep the magic alive for your children.

The Power of One Small Step

Write down one practice you learned or were reminded of in this chapter that you will use this week to live more fully in integrity. I started by telling the truth, even about small lapses, no matter how uncomfortable I felt.

Principle #5 Transform Your Life with Gratitude

appreciate your way to joyful parenting

> Gratitude is the most
> passionate transformative force
> in the cosmos.
>
> — SARAH BAN BREATHNACH

Our fifth principle, Gratitude, may seem like "fluff" at first glance, but it asks us to make a fundamental and profound change in how we express our love and appreciation to our child.

"Remember to turn off the shower and wash out your swimsuit, Ali," the mother said to her five-year-old in the shower stall next to mine. "Okay, Mommy," replied the girl. Her mother then walked into the next room to get dressed. A few minutes later I emerged from the shower at the same time as the little girl. Her mother approached and in a firm voice asked, "Did you turn off the shower?" "Yes," the girl replied. "Did you rinse your suit?" "Yes." "Did you remember to get the shampoo?" "Yes." Her face softened and she bent down, hugged her daughter and said, "Oh, Ali, Mommy loves you so much!"

With her words and facial expressions, this mother communicated a powerful message: I will appreciate and accept you when you do what I expect. Clearly, I have no idea how this mother usually relates to her daughter or how often she engages in conditional acceptance. However, if this example is typical of how she expresses her appreciation, this child is receiving a disturbing message: that what she does is more important than who she is (her essence).

When we appreciate our children (and spouses) for who they are, apart from their deeds, they feel closer to us and better about themselves. Appreciating the essence of a person is one of the five appreciation practices that can bring you more peace, joy, and connection. In fact, appreciating is the most effective connecting practice. People cannot help but feel closer to us when we genuinely and frequently appreciate them.

THE ART OF APPRECIATION

When we make appreciation a way of life, we:

- **BRING OUT THE BEST IN OTHERS: What we focus on grows. When we consciously focus on someone's positive qualities, we help draw out more of that.**

- **RAISE APPRECIATIVE CHILDREN: When parents complain about their unappreciative children, I ask, 'Do you model appreciation?" Invariably, parents flash a smile of recognition. It's easy to forget Gandhi's advice to 'be the change we wish to see in the world," yet that is exactly what it takes to effect change. Be the change you wish to see in your home.**

- **IMPROVE OUR HEALTH: According to a report published in Integrative Physiological and Behavioral Science (1998), researchers at the Institute of HeartMath of Boulder Creek, California, devoted to studying the heart, asked 30 people to focus on feelings of love and appreciation whenever they began to feel angry or frustrated. After a month, the researchers measured the participants' levels of DHEA, the anti-aging hormone, and found it had increased 100 percent, while levels of cortisol, a stress hormone, had decreased 20 percent.**

To master this art, you must acquire two distinct practices: First, establish your own appreciation rituals. Second, extend your appreciation to your child. Here are five ways to develop both practices:

Appreciate in Writing

Establish Your Practice

Written goals, affirmations, or statements of gratitude have the most creative power because we are more clear and focused when we write than when we merely think. Statements of gratitude, thank you notes, e-mails, and letter-writing exercises are some of the specific things we can do to enhance our own gratitude practice.

Several years ago, I started expressing my appreciation in writing and changed my life as a result. At that time, the book *Simple Abundance* by Sarah Ban Breathnach came out and several of my friends jumped on the *Simple Abundance* bandwagon. They created the gratitude journals promoted by the author and wrote in them every night. They couldn't believe that I was not joining them on their latest personal growth adventure and bugged me about it all the time.

I was up to my ears in overwhelm at the time and not interested in taking on any new practices. We were in the process of building a new home and had moved into our garage. Two adults, two children, an ant farm, and a dog: living in the garage. This was my husband's idea. He wanted to be on the property 24/7 and avoid the expense of renting an apartment for six months. "Besides," he said, "it will make a good story to tell our grandchildren." He, however, was not the one trying to entertain and care for two toddlers in the space where we used to park our cars. I was somewhat amused at first but after a few months, my nerves were wearing thin. My friends' standard reply to my woes was, "Gratitude journal. You have to get the book and start a gratitude journal."

Then one day I hit bottom. I heard my child's screams coming from the trailer that we used for a bathroom and ran to get her. I found her in the bathroom standing in a pile of broken glass.

A nail gun from our nearby building site had misfired and the nail had hit the window. I wish I could tell you that I then approached my husband with love and understanding. But, at that particular moment, I could not manage to be like Jesus or the Buddha.

Later that night it rained, and water seeped into the garage along with some earth creatures. When I got up in the middle of the night, I stepped on two night crawlers—in bare feet!

My friend Leah called the next day. When I told her about my experiences and state of mind, she said . . . you guessed it, "gratitude journal." So I succumbed to the messages (that I'm now sure were Divinely inspired) and went out that day and bought the book. Shortly after, I started my own gratitude journal—a simple notebook where I wrote down five things I was grateful for each night.

The first night, I was so upset about our living situation that I strained to find five things to write. *This is sad,* I thought, knowing that I had a life many would envy. Since I do believe in the power of a practice to change my life, I stuck to it. I committed to writing five things in my gratitude journal every night, no matter what. Some nights I was so tired, I would fall asleep mid-sentence. At times my writing was poetic. At times it was dull. But I made myself do it for 30 days. By the end of the first month, my life had started to transform.

Each day I would search for things to write in my journal. Since I was actively looking, I attracted more positive experiences. Soon I experienced garage living as more of an adventure than a pain. As a result of my gratitude practice, I have continued to attract an abundance of wonderful people, experiences, and material items into my life. My attitude has become a lot more positive and appreciative as well.

Appreciate Your Child

Words of appreciation are wonderful indeed. Written words of appreciation are experienced long after the spoken word. In my family, we write love notes to one another and have a special place to leave them. Write an appreciative note and slip it into your child's lunchbox. Send an e-mail into the inner sanctum of your teen. I heard of one mother who routinely wrote thank you notes to her children and that became second nature to them as well.

On the other end of things, if you don't receive thank you notes when you think you should, appreciate the joy you received when doing or giving whatever it was you think you should be thanked for. One friend, who stayed in touch with her stepsons following the divorce from their dad, found herself feeling resentful when the boys, who lived at some distance, didn't thank her for the birthday checks she sent. Then she read *The Holy Man*, a wonderful parable by Susan Trott, in which one of the characters is "the grandmother who never received thank you notes" and recognized herself. She decided then and there to drop her resentment and appreciate how much she loved these boys and make that experience complete in itself.

Appreciate in Advance

Establish Your Practice

To be most effective, gratitude needs to be expressed in advance. Dr. Ernest Holmes, founder of Religious Science and author of *The Science of Mind*, taught this truth through the process called Spiritual Mind Treatment. "Treatment" as it is termed, involves offering an affirmative prayer for attracting more of whatever it is you want. The treatment process includes declaring a truth you have realized, and then expressing your gratitude for the good that you know is on its way to you. What might you give thanks for right now in advance of its arrival? I'm giving thanks for the publication of this book and for being able to have a balanced, connected life with my family while traveling all over the country to speak about it.

Appreciate Your Child

You'll bump up the level of peace at home by appreciating your child before he performs a desired action. When you encounter even a tiny shred of what you want to see, express your appreciation. It's like fanning a flame. Children tend to rise to our view of them.

Appreciating magnifies. If you want to raise a child to be helpful, search out times when she shows the smallest inclination toward helpfulness and show your appreciation.

Appreciate the Essence

Establish Your Practice

Love yourself unconditionally, appreciating your essence. Love yourself for being who you are. Love yourself for wanting to become a better parent. Love yourself for you, not what you do. Appreciate the essence of others in the same way. I think one of the reasons we like to hear stories, hear speakers, or experience entertainers is that we get a taste of the unique essence of each person. Find something essential to appreciate about everyone, especially people you don't care for.

Appreciate Your Child

Appreciate who your children *are* more than what they *do*. Appreciate their *essence*. Rather than say, "I appreciate how quickly you cleaned up your room," say, "I appreciate how you kept your word about cleaning up your room. You did what you said you'd do, and wow! You did it so quickly!" When you appreciate a child's behavior, they like it. When you appreciate their essence, they *glow*.

Replace Anger and Frustration with Appreciation

Establish Your Practice

There is a bigger picture. We just can't see it sometimes, especially when things aren't going our way. The Sufis say, "When the heart grieves over what it has lost, the spirit rejoices over what it has left." However, sometimes it's hard to become like our spirits. When we feel frustration rather than gratitude, what we want is often being withheld from us by our negative thoughts. The practice of appreciation raises our vibration to a more positive level, and positive vibrations attract positive experiences. When we express gratitude, we affirm that a thing has already been experienced and create the environment in which it can occur and expand.

If you are having problems with someone, spend five minutes a day appreciating and being thankful for his or her good qualities. You can do this during meditation, or even while driving to work. You can also silently appreciate and express thanks for a person's difficult qualities or the conflict you are experiencing. As you give thanks, you may become aware of what you are learning from the experience or relationship, suggests Diane Goldner, in her article, "Opening the Heart," *New Age Magazine* May/June 2001.

Jack belonged to a men's group, and Phil, one of the other participants, really got on his nerves. The guy needed a lot of help, in Jack's opinion, and his mannerisms and behavior distracted the group. One day, Jack decided to appreciate Phil instead of feeling bugged by him. At the next meeting, when Phil spoke, Jack turned his body toward him, leaned forward, and listened. He thought, "I've been as crazy as Phil sometimes, and I'm going to appreciate and love him as if he were that crazy part of me." Soon Jack noticed that Phil didn't bother him as much. In fact, he began to look forward to and enjoy this practice with Phil. He then began using this technique in other settings, with similar results.

Appreciate Your Child

When you become upset with your child, insert a sentence of appreciation before dealing with the upset. If your family room has been transformed into a very messy arts and crafts center, appreciate your child's creativity (first to yourself, then to your child) before dealing with the mess.

Appreciate Often

Establish Your Practice

Several years ago, I bought a guided meditation tape about manifesting your desires. Side one of the tape featured exercises to use in the morning to attract what you want. Side two featured evening exercises for expressing gratitude. After a few weeks of this practice, I noticed that I was simply too tired in the evenings to complete the gratitude portion of the manifestation process. I did continue with the attracting exercises, and guess what? I was not manifesting nearly as much as I had in the early weeks. I had fallen into a common pattern. I was putting a lot of energy into expressing my desires and very little energy into expressing appreciation for what I did have. I was out of balance. It's a lot like having only one window open. For the breeze to blow through, it needs another channel.

Appreciate Your Child

Make sure you express some form of appreciation to your child everyday. I try to average five appreciations a day for each child. I'm not always successful, but over time this practice has become so automatic, my overall average is pretty close.

I recently witnessed a delightful example of appreciation in the grocery store, where I observed the following conversation between a father and his 12-year-old boy:

SON: Dad, calcium is good for your bones, right?

FATHER: Yes.

SON: Milk has calcium in it, right?

FATHER: Yes.

SON: Chocolate milk has milk in it, right?

FATHER: (with a smile of recognition): Yes.

SON: Then can we buy some chocolate milk?

FATHER: (in a friendly voice): That was really good negotiating, son. No, I'm not going to buy chocolate milk.

What an encouraging communication! This father took the time to acknowledge his son's good negotiating skills before interjecting a negative.

A FEAST OF APPRECIATION

Children learn by doing. That understanding, along with my desire to create a meaningful holiday ritual, gave me the impetus to come up with one of our favorite family traditions: the Thanksgiving altar. In years past, the meaning of this special holiday seemed to get lost among the food preparations and social events. I wanted to not only model appreciation but to have my children actively participate in offering gratitude.

I knew that if I sat down and announced a new tradition, I would meet with resistance or, at the very least, rolling eyeballs, so I just did it. I created a lovely sign that read "Thanksgiving Altar" and put it above the living room window ledge (our straw bale home has generous 18-inch window ledges). Three days before Thanksgiving, I placed a few items on the ledge and waited for the children to ask about it. When they arrived home from school they asked, "What's this?" "Our Thanksgiving altar," I answered in a joyful, detached tone. "What do you do?" they asked excitedly. "You place items on the altar that represent what you are grateful for. We will leave it here until Thanksgiving day as a reminder of all the things we have to be grateful for."

As the days went by, all of us filled the altar space with everything from photos of friends and relatives to a pair of tiny kids' skis that represented the mountain life we so love. The altar made our appreciation tangible. It made an abstract concept into something that our children would see, feel, and touch. The Thanksgiving altar remains one of our most potent appreciation traditions.

Offering sincere appreciation is a potent practice for invoking the power of the Law of Attraction. What we focus on grows. When we appreciate, we notice what we have. By focusing on what we have, we attract more of that into our life. So appreciate often and genuinely.

Prayer/Affirmation

Thank you.
Thank you.
Thank you.
Thank you.

Soulful Reminders

- When we make appreciation a way of life, we bring out the best in others, raise appreciative children, and improve our health.

- To master this art, you must acquire two distinct practices: First, establish your own appreciation rituals. Second, extend your appreciation to your child.

- Express your appreciation in writing.

- To be most effective, gratitude must be expressed in advance.

- Appreciate the essence of a person, not what they do.

- Appreciate often.

The Power of One Small Step

Write down one practice you learned or were reminded of in this chapter that you will use this week to bring more appreciation into you life. I started by focusing on appreciating my child's essence more than what she did.

Principle #6
Create
Abundance

live
prosperously

When you redefine your boundaries,
you re-divine yourself.

**— THE COUNCIL OF LIGHT
AS ASSIGNED ON THE SIRIAN PLANE OF LIGHT**

" . . . On a little creek of the sea, there lived a poor fisherman called Arsheesh, and with him there lived a boy who called him Father. The boy's name was Shasta. On most days Arsheesh went out in his boat to fish in the morning, and in the afternoon he harnessed his donkey to a cart and loaded the cart with fish and went a mile or so southward to the village to sell it. If it had sold well he would come home in a moderately good temper and say nothing to Shasta, but if it had sold badly he would find fault with him and perhaps beat him."

— C.S. LEWIS

FROM THE HORSE AND HIS BOY,
THE CHRONICLES OF NARNIA, BOOK 3

Sometimes my students wonder why I've made Abundance one of the principles for parenting with soul. Somehow they don't seem related. I made the connection in 1994, a year of extreme scarcity for me. When I looked for help, one of the resources I came across was a book called, *I've Been Rich, I've Been Poor, and Rich is Better* by Judy Resnick. And I thought, *I've had the state of mind of being a wealthy parent and I've had the state of mind of being a poor parent, and I'm a nicer mother and far more centered when I have financial freedom.* I'm not talking about extravagance. I'm talking about the freedom money gives me to be a better mother because my brain is more freed up to connect with my children and to nurture them. When I'm not in survival mode, there's more peace at home because I have peace of mind.

Money truly is only one form of abundance. I had a year of my life where I had very poor health, so I can tell you from experience that without health, money means absolutely nothing. Actually without health, nothing else meant anything. So money's only one form, but it's a form that gives us a lot of freedom. And if we can master our consciousness around this very emotionally charged form, all the other areas of life will benefit.

One of the keys to financial freedom is an attitude of abundance. Read the following statement out loud: "I have the power to manifest anything I want." Notice how you feel as you hear that statement. If you feel bad, tense, or get a "No way!" message from your subconscious, that may be your poverty consciousness speaking. If you thought, "Yes! I can do it. I can create anything I want," you probably have a pretty healthy consciousness of abundance.

THE THREE GREATEST MONEY MYTHS

You truly can manifest anything you want: an abundance of time, an abundance of money, an abundance of health, and an abundance of loving relationships. The problem is that most of us grew up around a lot of negative messages that were just the opposite of this idea. The first thing we have to do is bust some of the myths we've heard all our lives.

THE THREE GREATEST MONEY MYTHS

- Money doesn't grow on trees
- There isn't enough
- Money is the root of all evil

Myth #1:
Money Doesn't Grow on Trees

Who the heck came up with that? Did you know that the U.S. is the only country in the world with completely green money? Our forefathers wanted to create dollar bills that were representative of the abundance of Mother Earth. The original dollar bills were made from hemp, which is a very strong fiber, so money actually *does* grow on trees. Well, they grow on bushes. You can see that I'm getting a little silly here, and it's important to lighten up on this topic our culture has made so serious.

Myth #2:
There's Not Enough

Metaphysical teacher and visionary Gillian MacBeth-Louthan tells us:

> "When you say 'I don't have enough money,' whether it is fact or fiction, you completely downsize your money consciousness. This affects the next frequency of money that was coming towards you. The money screeches to a halt, no matter what format it was in. It turns around and goes the other way because you have given it the high sign verbally that it is not welcome. With each spoken word of such limited thinking, you send the frequency of money high-tailing it back into the cosmos. All energies and all subatomic particles believe your every word. Your world sees you as God. The molecules of everything see you as God. They view the truth of you. As a God-unit, they believe your words, your thoughts, your utterings, and your mutterings. You are the commander and chief of all life."

Pretty powerful words! And a wonderful example of the Law of Attraction. If we took all the money in the world and divided it equally among everyone on the planet, do you have any idea how much we'd each get? When I ask this question in my parenting classes, guesses usually range from $100,000 to a little over a million dollars. The real answer: *10 million dollars.* There is enough. There's also enough time, love, health, friends, great houses, and anything else we're looking for.

Myth #3:
Money Is the Root of All Evil

Many of us seem to think this is a quote from the Bible, but the actual quote is, "The *love* of money is the root of all evil." (I Tim 6:10) I really like George Bernard Shaw's version: "The lack of money is the root of all evil." When people get into extreme scarcity, that's when things get messed up, relationships get messed up, and when crime happens.

So now that we've busted the Three Greatest Money Myths, let's look at six key skills we need to live abundantly.

SIX PATHS TO ABUNDANCE

Because of the various challenges in my life around abundance, I have studied this topic extensively and offer a summary of the best thinking here. I've given my own names to these spiritual principles to translate them into the everyday world of parents.

SIX PATHS TO ABUNDANCE

1. Lights! Camera! Action! Imagine your way to success

2. Choose your most uplifting thought about Range Rovers

3. Trust and believe you will get what you want

4. Get your hand off the cabinet door

5. Take the next logical step

6. Bless those who have what you want

1. Lights! Camera! Action!
Imagine Your Way to Success

Images go right past the conscious and speak to our subconscious, which is the part of our brain that attracts everything we have in life. I was introduced to this concept in one of my favorite sitcoms as a child, *The Courtship of Eddie's Father*. For me, this was a show about a wealthy bachelor who dated lots of different women. The following situation is how *I* remember the dialogue going:

> One day Eddie's father came home and in front of Mrs. Livingston, his housekeeper, said, "I have had it with women! I do not want to talk to another woman, I don't want to see another woman, and I do not want another woman in my life ever again."
>
> And so the days start clicking by, no phone calls, no women coming over. The bachelor said to Mrs. Livingston, "I can't believe it. I haven't seen anyone. No one has called me. No one's come over. I don't understand what's happening in my life." And Mrs. Livingston says, "Oh, sir, I threw out your book and when women call on the phone I said no, no you cannot speak to him, he does not want to talk to women and I hung up. And when they came to the door I said, oh no, oh no, he does not want to see any women. You must leave right now. Goodbye."
>
> "Are you crazy?" he said. "What on earth made you do that?" she answered. "But sir, you said you never wanted to see another woman as long as you lived."

Just as he had Mrs. Livingston, we all have an obedient servant in our subconscious. So, be careful when you give instructions to your inner servant who may have no way of knowing how serious you are about your instructions. Imagine your way to success— it's one of the fastest ways to get there. Visualize it, feel it, see it very vividly. Feel good about it.

I experienced astonishing results almost immediately after starting a prosperity consciousness practice that involved imagination. It all started on New Year's Eve 1994. I was fifteen pounds overweight after having my second child, and had fought off eight different infections during the year, including pneumonia. I hit bottom when I went to the grocery store one November morning and had to charge my groceries because we had no money. I got really motivated really fast to do things differently. I began reading and talking with friends about money and prosperity. In December, my friend Sara said, "You've got to do this collage thing." I said, "Oh collage, smullage, that does not bring money." At the time, my husband was a waiter and worked on New Year's Eve and she said, "I'm coming to your house and we're going to do these collages because this book says it works." She was describing a technique some people call "Treasure Mapping."

That evening Sara and I set our intentions for the upcoming year and then tore pictures from magazines to represent what we wanted. Mine was covered with pictures of money. I glued the phrase "plenty of time" at the top and a photo of myself in the center. I also had a picture of a tropical beach, because a vacation to a place like this was really high on my list.

On January 1, 1995, I hung the collage in my bedroom. Life continued to bring a number of challenges. Sara kept saying we were going to manifest all these things, and at that point in my life, all I was trying to manifest was a shower each day because I had a newborn. I would look at the collage and practice what she said about feeling good every time I looked at it. I'd study it and say, "Ah, the ocean. Ah, wouldn't that be nice?" I looked at it and I allowed it to inspire me. I allowed it to help me feel good.

Fast forward to April 16, 1995. My husband, the waiter, was also a ski instructor and we attended a big end-of-the-season party for all the ski instructors on Aspen Mountain. We bought a bunch of raffle tickets for a drawing on two round-trip tickets anywhere American Airlines flies in the Caribbean. You had to be present to win. Around 3:00 that afternoon I said, "Honey, we've got to go. We have to go pick up the kids from daycare." And he said, "No, I'm going to win the prize. I'm staying." We got into a fight and I said, "Don't be ridiculous! That would mean you'd have to take a bus." He said, "Bye. I'm staying because I'm going to win."

So I went down the mountain and got the kids, which took about an hour and a half. When I arrived home, I saw a pile of cash on the dining room table and sputtered, "What's, what's going on?" He grinned and said, "Dig to the bottom." I dug to the bottom and pulled out a gift certificate for two round-trip tickets anywhere American flies in the Caribbean. Not only did we get a free trip to a tropical destination, we got all the cash from the raffle sales to spend on our vacation. To top it off, we had a time-share to use as well.

That was one of the most dramatic results of visualizing abundance through my Treasure Map. The most personally inspiring result that year, though, was my improved health. I experience perfect health now. I have not taken an antibiotic or drug of any sort since 1995. I hope you believe that you *can* have anything you want:

- **Time with your family**

- **Time alone**

- **Recreation**

- **Friends**

- **Joy**

- **Health**

- **Support**

- **Hugs and loving touch**

- **Wisdom**

2. Choose Your Most Uplifting Thought About Range Rovers

The Buddha tells us, "We are what we think. All that we are arises with our thoughts. With our thoughts, we make the world." Would you agree that your thoughts attract your experiences?

A lot of us look upon what we want and feel discouraged by the fact that we don't have it. One of the places I was tempted to choose an unproductive thought was when I was observing others who had what I wanted. After starting my prosperity practice, I noticed I would feel bad when I would judge others for being abundant.

I lived in a broken down house in 1994. This was a 30-year-old modular home bordering on dangerous. One of my husband's friends came to visit and pulled up in a Range Rover. I felt a sinking feeling, accompanied by a sinking thought *My house is not good enough, and I could never afford a Range Rover.*

I hadn't yet heard Abraham-Hicks' advice to "Offer only those thoughts and words that are in the direction of what you want," but I sensed that I needed to think more powerfully. I decided to change that around and said to my husband, "We can afford a Range Rover." He looked at me incredulously. "What are you talking about? We can afford a Range Rover? We cannot afford a Range Rover." I said, "Oh, yes, we absolutely can." He said, "You're deluding yourself with all this spiritual stuff." I said, "Let's think about it. We could sell the house. We have about $60,000 equity and a Range Rover's around $50,000. We could have a Range Rover." The fact is that you can have just about anything you want. It just depends on what you're willing to trade for it.

One way to keep words uplifting is to make sure in your conversations with yourself and with others that you say things like:

- "I choose not to."

- "I choose not to buy a Range Rover; I choose to have a home."

- "I choose not to go on vacation; I choose to buy a new sofa."

- "I choose not to order this new dress; I choose to go out to dinner."

3. Trust and Believe
You Will Get What You Want

When we trust, we're saying to the universe, "Yes! I believe I can partner with you to create what it is I want." My children taught me a big lesson about trust. When my older daughter was about three, I was watching some of her friends. Mid-morning the girls said, "We really want some milk." I had gone to the store that morning and bought two gallons. They sat at the table and I went around the corner to the kitchen and poured three glasses. I grabbed two glasses and brought them to the girls, saying, "Here you go," and as I turned to walk back, I heard the Wailing Wall.

"Who doesn't get one?"

"How come I don't get one?"

"No, that one's mine!"

"No, that's mine!"

I felt dumbfounded. I thought, *I have how many gallons of milk? If you kids drank all the milk that I have in my refrigerator you'd be sick.* Here they are in scarcity mode and all I've got to do is just walk back to the kitchen and get the third glass and bring it out. I thought *This must be how God feels. We're all whining and crying and every time we whine and cry we're pushing it away and pushing it away when there is such abundance. There is such abundance available to us if we only will trust.* The universe says, "Let's give it to that man. He knew it was coming. He's ready for it. He's going to allow it into his life." So trust the universe. Remember what it says on our money: "In God We Trust." Say it each time you handle your bills or hand them over.

When we do not trust the universe, we're in effect saying we don't believe we can have the life we want. To help you get into a mindset of trust, imagine some place you drive to regularly, like work or your child's school or daycare center. On your way, do you ever say, "What if the building's not there?" Sounds absurd, doesn't it? It is absurd and it's equally absurd to not trust the goodness that's available to you, too. Use this familiar building as a reminder and tell yourself, "The building's there and my abundance is here as well."

The trick with trusting is to get *general* in our wishes and desires. When we get too specific, we actually limit the good the universe can bring us. Keep it general:

- **"I want a car that's safe."**

- **"I want a car large enough for my whole family."**

- **"I want a car that's stylish."**

Maybe you want a car that's red. If that statement has you answering "yes," make that your affirmation. If you feel discouraged as you say those words, back off your desires and make them more general. Be as specific as you want as long as thinking of your desire inspires you. Maybe your car needs four-wheel drive because of where you live. Otherwise, keep it general: comfortable, safe, and affordable. Don't limit yourself to having to purchase the car; let the universe deliver it to you through the raffle at the ski company.

Be specific enough that you feel good, as specific as you can be, while remaining detached. Six years ago, a friend wanted a Honda van. When she saw one with a for sale sign, she called her husband. "Call them. This is the one I want. This is the one I manifested." And she didn't get it, which made her crazy. As it turned out, there was one waiting for her in Denver and it was even better—blue, which is what she wanted.

Three years later, Winnie, my cowriter, was helping me on a major book project when she had to go out of town for four days on family business. "I need to manifest a laptop, and it's not in my spending plan until later in the year," she mentioned one day when we were on the phone. "That's very interesting," I said. "My brother-in-law has an extra one he just offered to me for the next few months and I told him I didn't need it." Within days the laptop arrived at her door and she was able to keep up with her work while attending to her family.

When I put that picture of a tropical paradise on my Treasure Map, all I could imagine was that we had to write out a check or pay the money to go on a trip. But when I let it go and said, "The beach, oh, the beach. That would just be great," the universe delivered it in a completely unexpected way.

In their book, *Creating Money,* Sanaya Roman and Duane Packer tell about a woman who lived in an apartment building with noisy upstairs neighbors. She believed in these principles and she felt she was practicing them on her neighbors, who were causing her the loss of one of the richest kinds of abundance—peace of mind. She pictured them quieting down, imagined the peace and quiet in her mind, but their noise continued. So she concluded she needed to move. She looked and looked and looked and could not find anything appropriate. She then backed off and focused on the essence of what she wanted: a similar apartment that's comfortable, convenient, and quiet. A week later her landlord called and said, "I wanted to let you know your upstairs neighbors are moving out. An elderly woman and her cat are moving in." So focus on the essence of what you want, not too specific, and let the universe deliver it to you.

4. Get Your Hand Off the Cabinet Door

My friend Tyler came over one day with her 18-month-old daughter Sonora. Sonora was having a delightful time standing in front of each one of my lower kitchen cabinet doors, leaning her hand on a nearby door for support, then opening and closing each door. At one point we heard grunts of frustration. She gave us a look that said, "Can't you see, I need help here!" She could not get the last door open. Her frustration was building. We giggled as we noticed that instead of placing her stable hand on a nearby door for support, she had it on the door she was trying to open! "Get your hand off the door," we coaxed. Then my friend turned to me and said, "I wonder how many times we do that to ourselves, not seeing how we are disallowing what we want."

Chuang-Tzu said, "Happiness is the absence of striving for happiness." If you're not getting what you want, ask yourself two questions: 1) How much desire am I summoning? 2) How much am I letting flow? We let it flow with a strong belief that we deserve and will have abundance and by speaking in the positive. Creating abundance requires comfort with the paradox of feeling your desire with every fiber of your being while letting go of strong attachment for attaining it.

5. Take Only the Next Logical Step

It's so easy to set up grandiose schemes for ourselves—sometimes to the extent that we miss the next logical step. We wish for millions of dollars without planning how we will make the first hundred. We visualize world peace before creating peace in our own home. We can get caught in the trap of visualizing a manifestation so far from where we are currently vibrating that it becomes difficult to just take the next logical step.

When my friend Alexis was moving from Silicon Valley to Aspen in 1999, she wanted a good value on a car that would meet her driving needs in the mountains. Information began to easily come her way. She learned that the best value for her would be a three-year-old car with four-wheel drive in excellent condition. A little bit of research on the Internet determined that only two manufacturers had produced four-wheel drive cars in 1996. After looking at the various models, she determined she wanted a Subaru Legacy Outback and a little more research showed that the average price for a car like this in excellent condition was $16,000.

Holding a clear picture of the essence of what she wanted and open to something even better, she began to mention this to her friends and discovered within days that her friend Robyn wanted to sell exactly that car and had determined the right price was $16,000. Both women had set the intention several weeks before that the car would change hands easily and at a fair price, never dreaming the other had what she wanted. In fact, the car was even better than Alexis had imagined, with a superior sound system and luggage cover, two features she would not have specified that have added pleasure to her driving experience.

6. Bless Those Who Have What You Want

Do you choose to be put down or inspired by other people's abundance? When you see someone out there who has what you want or appears to have what you want, do you feel uplifted by that? Do you say, "Thank you for showing me what's possible?"

Or do you say, "That's not fair?" It's only when we can really truly bless those who have what we want that we start attracting more of that into our lives.

When we react negatively to someone else's abundance, we're a lot like crabs (plus, we often sound crabby!). Seafood distributors have found a way to reduce the cost of shipping crabs. They no longer put lids on the boxes. That's because when a crab claws up the wall of the box, all the other crabs pull him back down. No one escapes. When you perceive someone else's abundance, choose an uplifting thought. *When I help you get up there, that shows me I can get up there, too.* So bless those who have what you want.

I mentioned our friend's Range Rover and the feelings it evoked in me about not having enough. When Range Rovers became prevalent in Aspen, I heard all these nasty Range Rover jokes designed to make owners look stupid or bad. My guess was that whoever started those jokes had been feeling as bad as I had before I started some recovery in my perspective and my thinking. One day at a Texaco station I was standing in the line to pay and the guy in front of me said, in a profoundly disgusted tone, "I pulled out on the highway and this stupid Range Rover just cut me off!" And I thought *Now, would he have said this about a Geo?*

There was something in his message that implied people who drive Range Rovers are mean-spirited and nasty. I told some of those jokes, too, because some of them were really funny. I noticed that, if we really listen to ourselves our inner God will speak, and I noticed, it did not feel good after a while to tell those jokes because I was really tearing someone else down. It's not that I really even wanted a Range Rover, but it symbolized a whole different level of affluence for me at that time.

So I devised this Range Rover blessing: "Thank you, universe, for providing this Range Rover as evidence of the abundance that's available to me." That's the secret Range Rover blessing. Now, fill in the blank with whatever you want:

- **"Thank you, universe, for providing this really successful man and his business as an example of what's available to me."**

- "Thank you, universe, for showing me this pregnant woman as an example of what's available to me."

- "Thank you universe for providing this woman who has no wrinkles as evidence of what's available to me."

DETAILS, DETAILS

To complete the story about winning the two round-trip tickets anywhere American flies in the Caribbean, we had to use them within 30 days. I got on the phone with American to book my free flight and there was blackout after blackout after blackout. I was on the phone for two hours. We're scuba divers so I started with Cancun and all the scuba diving places. Cozumel? How about Cancun? No. Grand Cayman? No. And then I started thinking, *Okay what's every Jimmy Buffet song I know: Aruba, Jamaica.* I was running out.

Finally, after two hours and twenty destinations, I said to the agent, "I just want a beach. I don't care." I began to wonder if we were going on this trip after all. She said, "Oh, I have space to Barbados." I said, "Is that an island?" "Yes," she replied. "Does it have pretty white beaches and warm weather?" "Yeees." "I'll take it." So she booked us to Barbados.

I hung up the phone, walked back into my bedroom, and was absolutely dumbfounded as I glanced at my collage and realized that the word I'd cut off the bottom of the beach picture so that it could fit onto my collage was *Barbados*. On my collage was a picture of the Crane coast in Barbados. I literally sat down and sobbed in front of the collage. I had manifested the exact place that had seemed like a dream only months before!

Do not underestimate the power of these steps. They have completely transformed my life. With patience and a strong belief in these universal principles, they will transform yours as well.

Prayer/Affirmation

When I feel abundant,
I attract what I want and I bring more joy
to my parenting experiences.

Soulful Reminders

- **You truly can manifest anything you want: an abundance of time, money, health, and loving relationships.**

- **Images go right past the conscious and speak to our subconscious, which is the part of our brain that attracts everything we have in life, so imagine your way to success.**

- **Choose your most uplifting thought when confronted with what you don't have.**

- **Trust and believe you will get what you want.**

- **If you're not getting what you want, ask yourself two questions: 1) How much do I desire this? 2) How much am I letting flow?**

- **Take the next logical step toward your dream.**

- **Bless those who have what you want.**

The Power of One Small Step

Write down one practice you learned or were reminded of in this chapter that you will use this week to create more abundance in your life. I started by making a Treasure Map and feeling good whenever I looked at it.

15

overcoming obstacles to prosperity

Pray that success will not come
any faster than you are able
to endure it.

— ELBERT HUBBARD

Abundance is such a big topic and important principle, we need to pay special attention to anything in its way. Parents who choose to walk a spiritual path are asking to see everything that needs to be healed in themselves. Gillian MacBeth-Louthan cautions us that when you walk into any type of spirituality, automatically all your "vows of poverty" are reactivated and initiated. She goes on to say that many of us believe that "to be godly, you must be poor, you must do without."

Maria Nemeth, Ph.D., author of *The Energy of Money,* refers to the resistance that comes up when we set our sites on living abundantly as "trouble at the border." Simply knowing this can be helpful so we can recognize it when it happens. Our negative thinking can be an example of "trouble at the border." The desire to take a nap instead of reviewing our portfolio can be "trouble at the border." Getting sick on the day you're moving into a larger house can be "trouble at the border." Our former, smaller self clings to the familiar and kicks up a fuss when we want to move on. Nemeth reminds us that, "money is just energy. It's the intention with which you use this money; that's what we are here to learn how to do: use money with clarity, focus, ease, and grace."

Gay Hendricks refers to the phenomenon of doing something to bring ourselves down when things are going well as "upper limits."

FLUSHING OUT OUR UNCONSCIOUS BELIEFS

We all operate with unconscious beliefs. In fact, most of our beliefs are unconscious and run our lives unless we're willing to become self-aware. Some of the myths about money and abundance we reviewed in the previous chapter take the form of unconscious beliefs. Other unconscious beliefs that affect our abundance might sound like:

- **I'm not good enough.**

- **Life is hard.**

- **I don't deserve anything.**

- **Life won't work unless I'm perfect.**

- **I'm stupid.**

- **You can't trust other people.**

- **I have to do this alone.**

- **Rich people are mean.**

Here's a good way to flush your unconscious beliefs about money to the surface, inspired by Sondra Ray, author of *I Deserve Love:*

I DESERVE WEALTH	
In this column, write "I deserve wealth" 100 times.	In this column, write down any feelings that emerge, bodily reactions, or words you hear yourself saying inside as you're writing in the left column.

The first time I did this exercise, one of the things that quickly appeared in the second column was, "You bitch." I was shocked into remembering negative comments I'd heard growing up about people with money. I specifically felt that women who worked were bad mothers, a belief I had to overcome if I were to follow my dream of bringing this book into the world.

Sometimes our unconscious beliefs pop out of our mouths in the heat of the moment. Most often, though, we feel the belief in our emotions and bodies, without words. If you've ever felt anxious in a department store or had a temper tantrum as you closed escrow, these are probably unconscious beliefs about not having enough.

Unconscious beliefs can take many different forms, and since most of these originated when we were small children, they usually have to do with survival. Money triggers survival issues. Our unconscious beliefs don't leave us completely, but if we're willing to face them, they lose their power over us. One of my friends uncovered a powerful belief that had three parts:

1. **I did it wrong (imperfectly).**

2. **I'm going to get into big trouble.**

3. **I'm going to die.**

I think many of us who are achievers dance to a similar background rhythm. When she got clear that these were the three waves of fear that had run her life and hovered behind every emotional reaction she had, she began talking about them to take their power away.

It can be too time-consuming to monitor your thoughts to unearth unconscious beliefs, so I recommend trusting the most powerful connection you have to spirit—your feelings. Negative emotions are your subconscious telling you to stop; that what you are doing is not in support of what your higher self wants, and our higher self doesn't want us to be run by unconscious beliefs. Or they may be saying I am now so vibrationally different from what it is that I want, that I am setting up a wall of resistance rather than a path of allowing. Your emotions tell you all you need to know. They tell you what it is you want and how much you are allowing to come to you. Notice where you're using your emotional energy.

TURN OFF THE PROJECTOR!

For some reason, we humans seem to automatically blame people and circumstances outside ourselves for our problems. We also project our own shortcomings onto something outside ourselves. When we blame, we put ourselves into a powerless frame of mind instead of moving forward to resolve the situation. By looking within and taking responsibility for the results in our lives, we move into a place of power. Here are three techniques I use to turn off my projector:

Ask Yourself, "How Did I Help Create This Situation?"

No problem or lack of abundance is created in a vacuum. It always requires participation by two or more parties. You may feel surprised at the answers you get when you ask yourself this question. One friend, who owned a business, began using this when clients were late sending their payments. She noticed almost immediately that when this happened, she had ignored her inner guidance and taken on a client that didn't feel quite right or was late herself paying a vendor.

Do Whatever You Think They Should Do

When we project, we have the opportunity to find out what we should do next: whatever it is we think the other person should do. If you feel someone in your life should be more generous, be more generous yourself. If you want to be paid back sooner, you pay back someone you owe sooner. If you think someone should manage his money better, find a way to better manage yours.

Pray for the Other Person/Situation

If you perceive that some person or situation is preventing you from realizing your goal, here's a visualizing technique I use. I learned it from www.lovecandoanything.com. If you have trouble visualizing and cannot see a clear image in your mind's eye, simply thinking about the image will also work.

- **Find a quiet place, take a moment to relax, close your eyes, and take a breath.**

- **Imagine the person or situation surrounded by love and light. Some people think of a blanket of pink light or a bright star pouring light and love onto the person or situation.**

- **Imagine yourself in the picture. See things happening with this situation or person in the way you would like it to be.**

- **Always see the end result as a win-win situation for everyone involved. Love works best if you come to it with a forgiving and generous spirit, wishing the best for all concerned.**

- **See yourself celebrating the success of using the power of love in your life. Imagine yourself with your best friend, laughing and celebrating your success. Combine this image with a feeling of joy and let it go.**

KEEP YOUR WORDS POSITIVE

Many people bolster their visualizations about abundance with powerful, positive affirmations then undo them with the negative remarks they make all day. Affirmations can be extremely powerful. If you present imagined material strongly and vividly enough, it will be accepted by your unconscious as real. If you imagine you are wealthy and successful you *will* convince your brain. You will soon start to look, breathe, walk, and talk like a rich person, a healthy person, or a person in a loving relationship. When I started my own prosperity consciousness program, I wrote down

40 affirmations every night. Some examples of these were:

- **Money flows easily and effortlessly into my life.**

- **I deserve money.**

- **I am abundant.**

I had heard it takes 28 days to change a habit or to change thinking, and I noticed on day 30 that nothing had changed. And then, luckily, I noticed something else: I was saying a lot more than 40 things during the day that affirmed poverty. I'd go to the mailbox and I'd say, "Oh, I can't believe all these bills. Look at all this. Why do they all have to come at one time? We can't afford this." Four negative affirmations, and it was only 10 A.M. Then I'd go through the day, saying:

- **"I don't have enough money."**

- **"Oh, no, honey, we can't buy that."**

- **"I guess we won't go on vacation this year."**

- **"Our car is getting so old. I'm afraid it's going to break down one of these days."**

Everything you say is an affirmation. Every thought you think is an affirmation. So, be very careful how you choose your words and thoughts. Once I noticed all the negativity coming out of my mouth and swirling inside my head, I began to replace these with more positive, uplifting versions. One of my favorites that I replaced right away was, "I can't afford it." And the fact is, I usually can.

How do you feel when you pay your bills? Do you focus on the money gushing out of your bank account, or do you feel grateful for all the products and services you've received? Bill paying time is a great time to use affirmations. Unity minister Stan Burnett-Hampson suggests lighting a candle, burning incense, and playing wonderful background music when you pay your bills. I've heard of people who have their checks imprinted with "Bless you!" or other positive wishes to the people and companies receiving their payments. Don't limit your affirmations to bedtime or in the morning. Say them all day long. Neale Donald Walsch believes that every thought is a prayer. Pray and affirm abundance.

The fact that you were able to purchase this book means that you are probably experiencing a level of abundance that 90 percent of the world cannot possibly imagine, so just start to notice it more. Just start to notice what you're really grateful for. Bless your next meal with your gratitude. Millions and millions of people strive just to get that each day.

TAKE THE CHARGE OUT OF IT

If you have a negative association with the words money or dollars—and most of us do in this culture—choose a different word. My husband and I call cash *dineros*. I have no attachment to that because I was not raised speaking Spanish, and this is mangled Spanish, at that. So we say, "How many dineros are in the account?" or "Bring your dineros over here." Or, "I'm going to dineros your paycheck when I go to the bank." Take the energy off of the word. This applies to other parts of life as well, like friends, sex, religion, or dieting. Choose a different word—something fun—for whatever it is you're focusing on to get some of the negative energy off it.

FOCUS YOUR ENERGY IN THE DIRECTION OF WHAT YOU WANT

Remember the formula for manifestation from Chapter Eleven: Attract What You Want?

Strong Feelings + Repetition = Manifestation

You'll notice it doesn't say strong *positive* emotions plus repetition, does it? We can use strong negative energy to deflect abundance. So if anyone asks you, "How are you doing on your goal? Have you achieved it?" You say, *(very excited)* "No, it's still unfolding!" Make sure your strong emotion is positive when you talk with others or repeat things to yourself. If I had looked at my collage and said, "Oh, I'm not ever going to get to go to the beach," I would have been pushing it away. When we make these collages in my Parenting with Soul class, one of the guidelines is that there are no negative comments while doing the collage. It's not allowed because we want to create what we want, not push away what we don't want.

DON'T CURSE THE AIRPORT

If you were going on a dream vacation to a remote location that required two or three different layovers, would you curse each airport as you passed through it? Or, would you excitedly antic-ipate your arrival at your destination? Would you moan and complain, or talk about your upcoming adventure? Which are the more uplifting thoughts/actions? When we're on our way to the level of abundance we imagine, we can slow our progress if we get bogged down in negativity at one of the stops along the way.

What if you currently lived in the middle-class suburbs and I were to tell you that you would eventually be homeless for over a year, living in a tent compound with other homeless people? What if I then told you that not only would you overcome the adversity of your living situation, but go on to write a bestselling series of books that would heal and uplift millions of souls? What if I told you that you would become very wealthy doing so? If you were guaranteed this outcome, would you be better able to embrace your homelessness?

We would probably all relax into our circumstances if we knew the positive outcome. The challenge is to relax into our circumstances when we *don't* know the outcome. What if I told you the circum-stances above were facts for a guy you might know? You guessed it, author, Neale Donald Walsch. So don't curse the airport.

P.S. We're always in the airport.

Prayer/Affirmation

People are often unreasonable, illogical, and self-centered.

Forgive them anyway.

If you are kind, people may accuse you of selfish ulterior motives.

Be kind anyway.

If you are successful, you will win some false friends
and some true enemies.

Succeed anyway.

If you are honest and frank, people may cheat you.

Be honest and frank anyway.

What you spend years building someone could destroy overnight.

Build anyway.

If you find serenity and happiness, others may be jealous.

Be happy anyway.

The good you do today people will often forget tomorrow.

Do good anyway.

Give the world the best you have and it may never be enough.

Give the world the best you've got anyway.

You see, in the final analysis it is between you and God,
it was never between you and them anyway.

— **MOTHER TERESA'S ADAPTATION OF THE
PARADOXICAL COMMANDMENTS BY KENT M. KEITH**

Soulful Reminders

- **Parents who choose to walk a spiritual path are
  asking to see everything that needs to be healed
  in themselves.**

- **We all operate with unconscious beliefs. In fact, most
  of our beliefs are unconscious and run our lives unless
  we're willing to become self-aware.**

- **For some reason, we humans seem to automatically blame people and circumstances outside ourselves for our problems.**

- **To turn off the projector:**
  - ⇒ **Ask, "How did I help create this situation?**
  - ⇒ **Do whatever you think they should do.**
  - ⇒ **Pray for the other person or situation.**
  - ⇒ **Keep your words positive.**

- **Focus your energy in the direction of what you want.**

The Power of One Small Step

Write down one practice you learned or were reminded of in this chapter that you will use this week to overcome one of your obstacles to abundance. I started by making my everyday language more positive so it wouldn't cancel out all the affirmations I did in the morning.

Principle #7
Infuse
Your
Life
with
Peace

16

happy couple, happy child

It isn't so much about staying married
for the sake of the kids.
Couples need to stay happily married,
if they can, in order to help their children.

— DR. JOHN GOTTMAN

Your relationship with your partner is the emotional glue that binds your family together. It's also the base for peace at home. A couple, now sitting on the couch in front of me had made initial contact months earlier wanting help with their five year-old daughter who was "acting out." After five or six coaching sessions over the phone, I felt perplexed. I had explored every possibility I could think of for this child's behavior. At the mother's urging, I had even visited their home and observed the mother and daughter in action.

After the home visit, the mother and father wanted to meet with me in person instead of continuing our sessions over the phone. In my office I observed a pattern that was impossible to detect without the physical presence of the couple. Over the course of the office session, the wife frequently flashed her husband looks of contempt and disgust nearly every time he spoke. Afterwards, the couple never returned to hear my insights and though I may never know the reason for this child's mean streak, I felt I had unearthed a big clue.

Children model the behaviors they see. Words such as, "Treat your friends like you want to be treated" and "be nice" fall on deaf ears when children observe the exact opposite of this between their parents. Would you wish for your children to have the same relationship you have with your spouse?

Children constantly monitor the emotional climate of the home. Even at play, they subconsciously take in data and make decisions about themselves and their lives. Here are just some of the decisions children are forming as they move through their day:

- **Marriage is _____.**

- **Families are _____.**

- **Husbands are _____.**

- **Wives are _____.**

- **Children are _____.**

- **I am _____.**

Most children have formed their answers to these kinds of questions—their self-concept—at around the age of seven. These decisions are changeable later in life, usually with great effort. Take a moment and put yourself in your child's place. How do you think your child would fill in the blanks?

Children emerge from childhood with this collection of decisions. These become the belief system, perspective on life, and paradigm that shape our adult lives. You already know this: abused children are more likely to marry abusers; happy children are more likely to attract happy relationships. So, how do we give our child the gift of a healthy relationship? The basic skills are the same ones we use to parent with soul. John Gottman, Ph.D., author of the *New York Times* bestseller, *The Seven Principles for Making Marriage Work,* has concluded that the behaviors that kill marriages are criticism, defensiveness, stonewalling, and contempt. Even more telling, he says that marriages need a five-to-one ratio of appreciation to criticism between the couple to stay healthy. A one-to-one ratio is usually a precursor to divorce! The wisdom of relationship experts and spiritual masters falls neatly into our old friend *PHIL:* Your partner needs to feel *Powerful, Heard, Important,* and *Loved.*

As Rudolf Dreikurs tells us, when we are feeling filled (emotionally), we thrive. Each and every human being, whether in a child's body or in a full-grown body, has to have these needs met in order to feel happy, healthy, and whole.

When children do not have these needs met, it surfaces as misbehavior. When children do have these needs met, *their* need to misbehave decreases. As Dreikurs tells us, "All misbehavior is communication. When children feel understood, valued, powerful, and loved, there is *no* need to misbehave." It's the same for adults. You can follow these principles to create a supportive, peaceful, and loving relationship with your partner, whether they are in your life today, in your past, or in your future. These principles also apply to your relationship with your ex, your future partner, the single parent communicating with extended family, or others who partner with you to raise your child. Every relationship sends messages to our children. Let's make sure they're healthy and happy.

HELP YOUR PARTNER FEEL POWERFUL

Each of us wants to have control, choices, and create our own destiny. Our self-esteem and our ability to make choices for ourselves go hand-in-hand. No one likes to be told what to do. In this balance of power, there's no room for mandates, demands, or ultimatums. We each crave sovereignty.

Avoid criticizing your partner in front of your children. We only distance ourselves when we criticize our partner in front of the children. Instead, if you strongly disagree with your partner's parenting methods, move to another room to discuss the matter. If one or both of you is angry, try waiting until you calm down to discuss the matter. It can be helpful to have a signal for these episodes.

In our house, we use the time-out hand motion. Sometimes the vigor with which one of us makes it seems as if it might be another sign, but it accomplishes its purpose. The discussion stops until we're both ready to continue with cool heads.

FOCUS ON WHAT *YOU* CAN TO IMPROVE YOUR PARENTING SKILLS

When you find yourself judging your partner, instead of blaming or lecturing, focus on what you can do to improve your parenting. Dreikurs said it best: "The less we know what to do, the more we know what the other person should do." When I first got trained to teach parenting courses, I came home to my husband with the complete lecture series on how to parent our child. At that time we were dealing with horrendous power struggles and temper tantrums in our three-year-old, which I now realize were made worse by our ineffective response to them.

So, after suffering through a few weeks of a tremendously strained relationship with my husband (due to my superiority trip), I committed to not say one more thing to him about how he dealt with our child's power struggles. I had unwittingly taken Carl Jung advice: "If there is anything we wish to change in a child, we should first see if it is not something that could better be changed in ourselves."

Instead, I put the *Redirecting Children's Behavior* book in the bathroom and wore out the pages, reading the section on temper tantrums. After several setbacks, I began to have meaningful successes with my daughter and one day my husband said, "What did you do to calm her down?" You can imagine my surprise and delight with his question. This time, I was wise enough not to give a lecture, but instead, in a detached tone of voice, just listed what I had done. I noticed him practicing the steps I had used and I definitely noticed the improvement in our relationship. This all happened because I decided to simply focus on what I could do to improve myself, rather than him. Adults, like children, learn primarily from modeling, not from a lecture series.

HELP YOUR PARTNER FEEL HEARD

The number one reason wives cite for taking their husbands to therapy is because they don't feel heard. Ten years ago, when I was overweight, sick, and massively sleep-deprived, I felt I was beyond the end of the proverbial rope. One night I turned to my husband and said, "I'm having a nervous breakdown."

I have friends who say that when their dry cleaning is late, but I had never uttered those words. When I said this I was serious. My well-meaning husband came over to me and kindly said, "No, honey you're not having a nervous breakdown. You are such a great mom and considering what you're going through, I think you're doing just great."

At this point am I feeling heard? As a result, do you think I then got quieter or louder? If you guessed louder, you're semi-right. I lost it! Though my husband's intention was to soothe my upset, he inadvertently made it worse. I felt disconnected from him because he did not acknowledge my very strong feelings. Ten therapy sessions and $750 later, I was feeling heard. We both learned skills to better hear each other.

The disconnection of the Subtle Attachment Disorder (SAD) epidemic affects couples as well as children. Many, if not most, of us were raised without the personal connection we craved from our parents, so we don't always know how to forge this link with our partner. When people don't feel heard, they either increase the noise level in their home or sulk away. I hope I can make the skill of helping your partner feel heard easier for you, and a lot less expensive than it was for me!

My friend Joan shared the moment she fell in love with her partner. They'd been dating for several months, and one morning over breakfast she wanted to tell him something that was bothering her. It was the first time she was bringing up a topic like this and she felt very uncomfortable. As she began to broach the subject, he immediately stopped eating, turned his chair towards her, looked directly into her eyes, and leaned towards her. She felt deeply touched by the intensity of his listening. She felt heard in a big way, and she'd barely started talking.

It's helpful to remember the power of silence. Sometimes silence is the most appropriate way to help our partner feel heard. When in doubt, take a breath and simply listen.

USE REFLECTIVE LISTENING

One of the simplest ways to help your partner feel heard is with Reflective Listening. You've probably heard the expression, MVP (most valuable player). If you master and use this technique, you'll become an MVE (most valuable everything). Well, that might be an exaggeration (only your partner can decide that), but MVE is how you remember these steps:

1. **Mirror: When your partner expresses something, paraphrase back to him or her what you heard. You can use phrases like:**
   - ➠ **"Let me see if I've got that . . ."**
   - ➠ **"I think I'm hearing you say . . ."**
   - ➠ **"So you're saying . . ."**

2. **Validate: Communicate acceptance of (not necessarily agreement with) what they're experiencing:**
   - ➠ **"I can understand why you feel that way because . . ."**
   - ➠ **"That makes sense."**
   - ➠ **"I see."**

3. **Empathize: Confirm that you've read your partner's feelings accurately. If he or she has already used feeling words, use a synonym if you can, rather than repeat their exact words:**
   - ➠ **"And I imagine you might feel . . . Is that it? Anything else?"**

HELP YOUR PARTNER
FEEL IMPORTANT

What's more intoxicating than receiving heartfelt appreciation? *Appreciate* means to increase in value and when we appreciate our partner, they feel more valuable. They feel important. We live in a society that focuses on what's wrong rather than what's right. So, it's second nature for most of us to do the same. Focusing on the problem has its place, but not in healthy, happy relationships. Speak your appreciation. As Abraham-Hicks says, "Go on a rampage of appreciation." Make a list of ten things you appreciate about your partner right now. Write appreciative notes (and give them to your partner). What you will get in return is a closeness you may have never dreamed possible.

Another way to show your appreciation is to write, "What I love about you" notes. Just for fun, write three things you love about your partner on a note everyday next week. Do this and watch your relationship move to a new level.

HELP YOUR PARTNER
FEEL LOVED

How can we learn to love our partners unconditionally? One way is to sincerely accept and appreciate your differences. You don't have to be carbon copies to become an effective parenting team. I went through a period of time when I was constantly complaining about how my husband was playing too rough with our girls. As their mother, I felt the need to jump in and object to his "rough-house" play, but the girls seemed mostly okay with it. After we discussed it further one day, I realized that it was not so important that we both treat the children exactly the same way. And in fact, I realized that there were benefits to the kids experiencing two different parenting styles.

Another way to connect is to make time for each other. When we make time for our partners, we are, in essence, saying, "You are important to me." I know how difficult it can be, especially if you have small children, to find the time to connect. But the price we pay for not connecting is high. Disconnection often shows up as feeling unappreciated, short tempers, and judging each other, not usually the values we are attempting to impart to our children.

Another idea for bringing you and your spouse together is to bring you and your spouse together—literally. It's called a "date." One goal could be to try and spend at least two hours away from the house with only your partner each week. If this seems like an impossibility, your next logical step might be to schedule a time to brainstorm about how you could make a weekly date happen. When you do brainstorm, don't focus on all the hurdles and limitations (you already know these). Commit to keeping the dialogue positive. These dates are important! They model "taking care of your relationship" for your children and keep *you* nourished. My husband and I started our weekly dates eight years ago and it continues to remain a joyous part of our life together.

CHOOSE BEING CLOSE OVER BEING RIGHT

In every interaction we have with anyone in our lives, we get to choose: Do you want to be close or do you want to be right? Gerald Jampolsky's version of this is, "Do you want to be happy or do you want to be right?" Which of those choices sounds more peaceful? If we have a close relationship with our partner, we'll have a happy one and happy children as well.

Giving up the need to be right can be a real challenge, especially for those of us who were first-born, or anyone who felt great pressure from our parents to be right. Make a sign that says, "Close or Right?" and place it wherever you most need to be reminded of this practice: on the bathroom mirror, on the refrigerator, or on the dashboard. Also, resist the temptation to remind others to choose being close over being right. Any step you take to enrich your relationship with your partner will benefit every member of your family. Gauge for your success as a couple right now. In the last 24 hours, how many minutes did you spend in loving eye contact? Physical touch? Overlooking minor irritations?

Appreciating? My best wishes to you and your beloved as you travel this most challenging of paths on your quest for growth and joy.

Prayer/Affirmation

I love in you what I love in me.

Soulful Reminders

- **Children model their parents' behavior: We can expect our children to demonstrate the level of respect, cooperation, and support they observe in their parents' relationship.**

- **If you find yourself blaming or judging your partner, focus on improving your parenting skills.**

- **Just like with your child, your relationship with your partner will thrive when you help them feel Powerful, Heard, Important, and Loved.**

- **Notice how often you choose being right over being close and choose to create closeness.**

The Power of One Small Step

Write down one practice you learned or were reminded of in this chapter that you will use this week to create an even more supportive and loving relationship with your partner. I started by focusing on *my* parenting skills instead of criticizing my husband's.

17

embrace what is: a recipe for peace

> This place where you are right now,
> God circled on a map for you.
>
> — HAFIZ

Can you imagine how much more peace we'd experience if we accepted life just the way it is?

When I was writing this chapter, I blocked out a whole week to work on this book. I'd done the grocery shopping, paid my bills, and hired someone to clean my house. I had no other obligations other than to fully use and enjoy the eight hours a day I'd liberated to create this book and be present and available to my family when they were home.

The first day, my older daughter stayed home from school, sick. *This is a setback,* I thought. I was a little stressed, but in a short time I somewhat gracefully accepted what was happening and made the best of the day (after all, I was writing a chapter called Embrace What Is). My children had never missed more than one day of school at a time. They are extremely healthy, so I felt sure that I could be fully present for her on this day and make up the lost time when she went to school the next day. Ultimately she stayed home sick for two weeks. A couple of those days, both girls were home sick.

I lost it.

Then on about day ten, tired of my negativity, I started looking for the gift in this challenge. I asked myself some pivotal questions:

- **How can I get centered around what's happening?**

- **How can I embrace what is?**

- **What is the gift here?**

After some thought and sitting in silence, I realized that this experience would give me the opportunity to do some things I had been putting off: cooking healthful meals, connecting with my daughter, slowing down, and returning overdue phone calls. In one connection-filled afternoon, my daughter revealed a hidden talent by helping me set up my entire filing system.

After accepting the gifts that came with being home with a sick child for two weeks, I remember wishing that I would have known the power of gracefully accepting reality years earlier. My second child weighed only five pounds when she was born, so she needed to be fed every hour and a half to two hours. I nursed constantly. For seven months (not that I was counting!) I never slept for more than two hours at a time. Forget deep sleep—no alpha waves happening here. As a result, I quickly slid into a semi-hysterical state of sleep deprivation. During the middle-of-the-night feedings, I became obsessed with the clock. Each time her cries awakened me I'd do my calculations and then agonize over how little sleep I'd gotten. Each time I laid her back into her crib, I'd suffer in advance as I estimated what time she'd wake me up again.

I felt no peace. Increasingly desperate and nearly insane with fatigue, I contacted La Leche League when she was five or six months old. They made a suggestion that changed my life. They told me not to look at the clock when nursing throughout the night. That way, they said, you don't use the feedback to make yourself feel worse. I went home, covered my clocks and immediately became more present. Instead of calculating how much sleep I hadn't gotten, I would say to myself *I am nursing my child* and focused only on feeding her, holding her, changing her diaper, and putting her back to bed. Within two weeks I felt like a different woman, even though my schedule had not changed.

As Eckhart Tolle says, "If you find your life situation unsatisfactory or even intolerable, it is only by surrendering first that you can break the unconscious resistance pattern that perpetuates that situation." I certainly experienced this truth. I started the path to embracing my reality when I surrendered to the fact that I had a problem and needed outside help.

Life happens. And when we decide to become parents, even more life happens. There's more stuff, more people, more activity, and more noise. And not all of it is what we think we want. Along with expanded love, joy, and laughter, we experience more disagreements, more anger, and more fear because our world has become bigger and more complex. The new world we've created can feel frustrating and scary.

Many of us wrestle with the dark side of parenting: the frustrations, our own shortcomings, the many inconveniences, and disappointments. The more comfortable and accepting we are of our present moment circumstances, the more effective we become. I'm inviting you to parent from a state of grace, which is timeless, present, and in the loving now. Some of these ideas may sound familiar. Some ideas may require a leap of faith. Any movement in the direction of embracing life as it is will increase the level of joy in your parenting experience. Reality is always temporary. Nothing remains the same, and your challenges will change as well. Embrace what is right now, like Byron Katie, who says, "I am a lover of reality. When I argue with *what is,* I lose, but only 100 percent of the time."

The initial step in learning to embrace what is involves is examining our relationships with the past, present, and future. One of my favorite slogans is from Alcoholics Anonymous: "Don't leave before the miracle." When we refuse to embrace what is, we're doing exactly that. We've marched down the road of our own view of the past or the future instead of hanging in the now.

FORGIVE THE PAST

The lack of peace we experience on a daily basis often has to do with our resentment and regret about the past. Becoming a parent often brings up strong feelings about the way we were parented. We may feel inadequate and unprepared for this new way of life. We may regret poor decisions that impacted our children. We may dislike some of the decisions our parents made. I invite you to forgive it all. Emmet Fox, a 1930s metaphysician, said it best: "When you hold resentment against anyone, you are bound to that person by a cosmic link, a real tough mental chain; you are tied by a cosmic tie to the thing that you hate. The one person, perhaps in the whole world, whom you most dislike, is the very one to whom you are attaching yourself, by a hook that is stronger than steel."

Ernest Kurtz, author of *Spirituality of Imperfection,* says, "To acknowledge, to accept, and to forgive one's parents—both what they gave and what they did not give, both one's dependence upon them and one's independence of them—is the ultimate hallmark of maturity." Ask yourself right now: Who do I need to forgive? Notice who pops into your mind. You might find it helpful to list the people who've hurt you, describe the offense in detail, share it with a trusted minister or friend, and then burn the paper. Many people report that this ritual seems to move the forgiveness process along.

Ben first encountered a version of this exercise in 1987, in a long weekend workshop, where the homework on Friday and Saturday nights was to list all the hurts that he had done to others and that others had done to him. The following day, he read it to someone he'd partnered up with, and on Sunday night the whole group participated in a burning ceremony. "I didn't want to do it," Ben reported sheepishly. "I'd worked hard to dredge all this stuff up. I'd committed, though, to do whatever it took to get my life on a better track, so I did it, but I was the very last person to drop his list into the burning bowl. I clearly saw how I wanted to hold on to all those grievances."

If you find you still can't let go of someone who's done you wrong, pray for them for two weeks. You'll almost always notice a shift. Sometimes it takes longer. Sometimes it takes a lifetime. And you may discover layers of forgiveness around a single incident. It takes what it takes. But set the intention to completely forgive everyone. I know I've gotten all the way to forgiveness when I feel gratitude for the original, hurtful experience—when I've seen the perfection in life's plan. That's when I've finally embraced what is for that situation.

Follow the advice of Abraham-Hicks: "Tippy-toe back into the past. Don't bulldoze." Learn and move on. The most important person to forgive is yourself. As a parent, I often fall short of the mark, but I keep going. I make it up to my kids, forgive myself, and move on.

YOU MUST BE PRESENT TO WIN!

Do you find yourself thinking of other things while your child is talking to you? Do you lose your patience easily? Ever feel like you are missing out on the richness of the parenting experience? If so, you may be in the habit of worrying about the future or living in a past that cannot be changed. As parents, our consciousness is scattered; we may be bathing our toddler, but our mind is wandering to the grocery list, the play date schedule, or the dinner menu.

We often entertain thoughts that have nothing to do with what's going on right now. Being present (or "mindful" in Zen Buddhism) is about placing all of your attention on the present moment. It's as simple as becoming aware of what you are doing *right now*. Make it your goal to hang in the present as much as possible, for it is here that you can cultivate calmness, patience, and connection. "Be here now," as Ram Dass urges us. It's a peaceful place. The fastest way to bring your mind back into the present moment is to take a breath or two or three.

At the pool, I overheard two 12-year-old girls; one of them had already learned this lesson.

> GIRL #1: Look at that lady's towel. It's cool;
> it says Hawaii.
>
> GIRL #2: Wouldn't you rather be in Hawaii?
> I'd rather be in Hawaii.
>
> GIRL #1: I'd rather be here, right now, with *you.*

What a touching demonstration of presence! *I'd rather be here with you than anywhere else.* What better way to help our children feel *Powerful, Heard, Important,* and *Loved?* How often do our children feel this level of presence from us? How often do we feel this from others? The frequency of this type of interaction in our lives largely affects the amount of joy we experience. Thich Nhat Hanh, in *The Miracle of Mindfulness* reminds us, "Our appointment with life is in the present moment."

RELEASE THE FUTURE

When parenthood wears on us, we sometimes fantasize about when our children will grow up and be out on their own, or we use our creative energy worrying and conjuring up elaborate negative scenarios. Both of these practices jolt us out of the peace of the present moment. Replace worry with trust or take action if a concern is valid. Trust or take action to soothe yourself back into the current moment. Hold positive expectations, but hold them lightly. Live now, in the present. It's the most powerful influence on the future.

WHAT'S NEXT?

A friend who taught drivers' education said the training films helped her change her view of driving (and life) from a challenge to a game. Instead of becoming angry when someone turned in front of her or frightened when a child ran into the street, she drove knowing something would happen and that her job was to be ready for it. When the unexpected happened, she felt delighted with her relaxed readiness—quite a change in perception!

The Buddhists have a "What's next?" orientation to life that reminds me a lot of that. Something changes. Our car suddenly goes into a skid. The engine overheats. The car in front slams on its brakes. If you play computer games, you're probably already familiar with this perspective. The first time one friend saw the game Tomb Raider, she remarked, "That reminds me a lot of my life." Instead of feeling as if you're being "done to," by events and outcomes, play it like a game. Consider life like a screen, across which march ever-changing scenes. Face them head on, with knees bent, always ready for the next thing.

MASTER THE ART OF ACCEPTANCE

Say "yes" to it all. Accept every event, every inconvenience, and every blessing in disguise—your child's feelings and your feelings. Experiment with everyday events, like a child slow to get out the door when it's time to go:

- **Accept that my child is dawdling.**

- **Accept that we'll be late.**

- **Accept that I feel angry.**

- **Accept that I have a need to look good.**

Roll with the punches. Go with the flow. I realize these are clichés, but clichés become clichés because they're so true. When we embrace what is, we lighten up. Make this poem your way of life:

Flow

BY
WINNIE SHOWS

Any clutching
slows the flow.
Any clenching

chills the chi.
Any clinging
loses grace.
Any closing
lessens me.

All removing
opens space.
All relaxing
lets me go.
All reflecting
slows my pace.
All releasing
makes it so.

One friend said she had a life-changing moment 20 years ago when she saw a bumper sticker that said, "Even if the world is falling apart, I can still have a good day." What a concept. Give yourself permission today to be happy, no matter what. As Meher Baba says, "Don't worry, be happy."

- **Even if my child is sick and the house is a mess, I can still have a good day.**

- **Even if I'm short of money, I can still have a good day.**

- **Even if I've only gotten three hours of sleep, I can still have a good day.**

- **Even if my child gets poor grades, I can still have a good day.**

- **Even if our family vacation is canceled, I can still have a good day.**

- **Even if my child is drinking and using drugs, I can still have a good day.**

I realize this is an outrageous idea in our "fix-it" culture. How can I have a good day if my child is destroying his life? Ironically, Al-Anon, Codependents Anonymous, and other support groups for people who love addicts, have found that our attachment to a problem exacerbates the problem. So you will actually help your loved one if you find a way to accept what is and focus on your own behavior.

Many of us practice "If, then" happiness, where we base our level of delight on some outer condition. When we drop the prerequisites and go straight for the joy, life works better. Tolle says that, "To offer no resistance to life is to be in a state of grace, ease, and lightness. This state is then no longer dependent upon things being in a certain way, good or bad."

I give you permission to have a good day, no matter what's happening. Follow the invitation of Abraham-Hicks to "Be as happy as you want to be in a world gone mad. Be as safe as you want to be in a world that is afraid of everything. Be as healthy as you want to be in a world that is mostly sick. Don't let the statistics that someone else has created affect you. 'Statistics' are only the results of how others are thinking. They are the calculated results of the way others are flowing energy. They have nothing to do with you. You get to choose—you are wise enough, smart enough, deliberate enough."

SAYING "YES" TO IT ALL

Anne told me about her 20-year-old manicurist, who seemed wise beyond her years. All day long she sat and listened to what her various clients had to say, and almost always her response was, "Uh, huh." Her clients felt listened to and liked her a lot. Therapists know this secret, too. By giving an accepting response like this, they create a safe space for their clients that promote healing. When we say "yes" to each moment of life (even if it's "Yes, this is what's up now," rather than "Yes! I'll take it!"), we create the space for it to become even better.

This is a practice that takes practice. Watch your words. Keep them positive and forward moving. Like many parents, I felt trapped at home when my children were little. It helped me a lot to ask myself, "How can I make the best of this situation?" and to tell myself, "If it's happening, it is the best thing right now."

Use words of acceptance. Change "I have to" to "I get to." You may want to adopt some affirmations like these:

- **Everything is unfolding appropriately.**

- **It's all perfect.**

- **Rejection is God's way of protection.**

- **God has a plan for me that's more wonderful than I can imagine.**

- **There's a gift here.**

Whenever someone has left Byron Katie's life, instead of feeling rejected, she says, "I've been saved!" Several single mothers I know have adopted that mantra instead of pining that they'll never find Mr. Right.

LAUGH YOUR WAY TO ACCEPTANCE

Laughter is a good indicator that we're accepting what is. How much laughter have you experienced today? How much happens in your home on a typical day? Can you laugh when life feels daunting? When you've been deceived? When someone's mistake nearly costs you your life? One of my favorite stories comes from Drs. Kate Ludeman and Eddie Erlandson in their book, *Radical Change, Radical Results:*

> When my husband, Eddie, and I first became a couple, we visited Fiji. One afternoon we went out kayaking, and though Eddie felt uncomfortable, I, who had more kayaking experience, assured him that kayaks were stable and that I had kayaked in 20-foot ocean swells without capsizing. As we neared some large whitecaps, Eddie said he felt uneasy continuing out to sea, but I insisted we'd be fine.
>
> Five minutes later, our kayak caught on the shallow reef beneath the whitecaps and overturned. We were

knocked underwater by the fierce waves and strong
undertow and repeatedly jostled against the reef.
Eddie rescued me several times as I was pulled under.
We finally freed ourselves and as we slowly swam
toward shore, bloody and injured, I felt angry with
myself for causing this life-threatening accident. I fully
expected anger and blame from Eddie. What I got
instead was uproarious laughter. He felt so delighted
that we were alive! He told me how much he appreciated my stamina, my grit, and that I hadn't panicked.
I think that was the moment I fell in love with him.

If you're struggling to embrace your current version of What
Is, you can create laughter to move you closer. On my Disneyworld
trip with my 18 Italian in-laws, I sometimes felt uncomfortable when
our noisy group would board a ride—especially the enclosed ones
like the Monorail. No one could be heard above our loud exchanges.
And the topics, which might range from someone's marital problems
to who had diarrhea on the trip, weren't particularly innocuous.

My sister-in-law had created official-looking name badges we
all wore. As we boarded one ride, preceded by our decibel level, someone asked what group we were. "Oh, we're Yellers Anonymous,"
I replied in a loud voice. "We're trying to learn to talk quietly."

Well, at least I laughed. And I definitely became more accepting. Our power and acceptance emanate from a place of joy. Step
back into that place as quickly as you can.

NO MORE VICTIMS!

When life feels challenging, it can be easy to feel like a victim.
Do everything in your power to avoid this mindset. It doesn't help
anyone, and it takes us a step further away from joy and creating
the life we want.

In their book, *Conscious Loving,* Gay and Kathlyn Hendricks
advise us, "Each time an event occurs, we have a choice of whether
to view it as what ought to have happened or what ought not to

have happened. Many people tie up enormous amounts of their energy in thinking that the events of their lives are not the ones that ought to have happened. They get into a victim position with life itself, so that they perceive that they are completely at the effect of a hostile universe. There is no positive payoff for seeing the world this way." And definitely no peace.

If you feel overloaded with parental responsibilities, remember the mantra of Carol Orsborne, founder of Overachievers Anonymous: "All I have to do is the very next thing." Our victim feelings sometimes come from future thinking. Simply take the next step and the one after that will become clear. When I felt mired in the quicksand of my child's two-week illness, I was reminded of the power of this mantra. I changed my thinking from *What am I going to do if this book is not finished on time! I can't do it. I'll be in trouble* to *The very next thing I need to do is fix breakfast for my child, call the doctor, be here now.* I could feel the tension lift as I developed a laser focus on only the next thing.

I do believe there's a divine plan for us all and the human part of us can't see the big picture, so we become discouraged when our efforts at creating the life we want seem to become derailed. But our higher self knows. In the words of English novelist and critic Storm Jameson, "For what I have received, may the Lord make me truly thankful. And more truly for what I have not received." Trust that life is unfolding in the best and highest way. Sometimes we can see this more clearly if we remember other crises, disappointments, and challenging times and notice how our lives changed as a result.

BEFRIEND THE ENEMY

Whenever I've taken the time to look back over the most difficult periods in parenting, I always see the same thing: that it ultimately led to something even better. Life expanded. I grew and I learned lessons that will serve me for decades. The challenge I experienced nursing my daughter led to a lifelong skill in being present. When my children had to share a room because we were remodeling, they developed a closeness that persists five years later. My extreme frustration about our living conditions while our home was under construction led me to my gratitude journal practice that continues to expand my capacity to appreciate.

On a piece of paper, take a moment to list the most painful and difficult events in your life and what resulted. I think you'll see the same thing.

The Painful Event	How My Life Changed

As astrologer Jonathan Cainer says, "To dislike the current situation is to dislike an airport terminal or a central rail interchange. These are not places that are designed to be lived in. Their whole, sole purpose is to provide a space that people can pass through on their way to somewhere else." Like I said before, don't curse the airport.

In 1989, my friend Winnie was experiencing what seemed to be one of the lowest points in her life. Hoping to gain some perspective, she purchased a journal with dragons on the cover and listed all the major traumas of her life and how her life changed as a result. To her amazement she saw for the first time how each event had played an important part in shaping who she was and leading her to an increasingly bigger life. The layoff at a small software company had led to a career in Silicon Valley where she doubled her income in three years. A friend's death had taught her to stay up-to-date in her relationships. A close relative's drug and alcohol use had started her on a spiritual path.

Winnie kept the dragon book for several years, adding one or two events a year, and now brings it out only occasionally. She's got the big picture. At some level we all know life is unfolding, as it should, but being human, we forget.

Befriending less-than-perfect circumstances means actively embracing them, making peace with them. In *The Power of Now,* Eckhart Tolle advises us to "Accept—then act. Whatever the present moment contains, accept it as if you had chosen it. Always work with it, not against it. Make it your friend and ally, not your enemy. This will miraculously transform your whole life."

Carl Jung's active imagination process offers a specific way to do this. Get into a relaxed state by taking three deep breaths. Imagine the present situation as a person or conscious thing. It could be a bogey man, a Sesame Street-type monster, or a ghost. Imagine what it looks like. Give it a name. Have a conversation with it. Ask it what it wants to tell you. You might be surprised at what you hear. Partner with adverse circumstances. Don't fight them.

Honor your current challenge. Build an altar to it in some form. One friend who struggles with money problems wears green and drinks green tea when she's short of cash. Joke about it. Pretend you asked for it (some spiritual masters say we have). Buddy up, and, yes, even love it. And love yourself for being willing to view adversity in a new way.

LOVE YOURSELF

For many of us, the hardest "what is" to embrace and one of the greatest obstacles to having the life we want is ourselves. Learn to love yourself and your life unconditionally, warts and all. Jung, the grandfather of depth psychology, said, "The most terrifying thing is to accept oneself completely." Ask yourself:

- **How can I love myself for losing my temper?**

- **How can I love myself for my messy house?**

- **How can I love myself for failing?**

- **How can I love myself for not having a clue sometimes?**

Be like a parent to yourself, loving and accepting what is. Take it a step further. If I want to be a patient parent, can I first love and accept myself for being impatient? Metaphysician Barbara Marciniak tells us, "[You create] inner peace and inner love by accepting who you are and all that you have done in life and all that has been done to you in life."

EXPANDING OUR HERITAGE

When we embrace what is, we make it easier for the next generation to do that, too. With embracing what is, comes resiliency—a critical life skill. We model this with our words, actions, and attitude. I find this out loud stream-of-consciousness approach helpful in showing my children my train of thought:

- **"Well, this road is closed, so we'll take the other one."**

- **"I forgot to buy milk, so let's have grilled cheese sandwiches for breakfast."**

- **"I used mean words with Daddy, and now I'm going to write him a note to tell him I feel sad about that and how much I love him."**

You will soon hear your own children using words like these. Remember *that* with every thought and word, and embrace what is.

Accepting every situation, human circumstance, and experience, creates an opportunity to release and a chance to end suffering. This is "letting go" in its highest form. When we lament, worry, and hold on to negative emotions over a situation, we miss a precious gem—the present moment. If we're harboring negative emotion, we're harnessing the negative creative power of the Law of Attraction. By modeling grace, we become a blessing to our children and teach them the concept of conscious creating. When you embrace what is, you literally step into a state of grace. And in that state, anything is possible.

Prayer/Affirmation

Dear God,
I release this business, project, or goal to You.
I know that my tension, my control, and my
Direction do not serve the project or You.
May my resources be used by You.
I ask only that Your will be done as I have felt
You have asked me to do.
And now I place all outcome in Your hands.
Amen.

— MARIANNE WILLIAMSON

Soulful Reminders

- Along with expanded love, joy, and laughter, we experience more disagreements, anger, and fear because our world becomes bigger and more complex when we become parents.

- Forgive the past.

- You must be present to win.

- Release the future.

- Adopt an attitude of "What's next?"

- Say "yes"to it all. Accept every event, inconvenience, and blessing in disguise.

- Laugh your way to acceptance.

- Refuse to be a victim.

- Befriend less-than-perfect circumstances.

- Most importantly, love and accept yourself.

The Power of One Small Step

Write down one practice you learned or were reminded of in this chapter that you will use this week to accept what is. I started by asking myself when things didn't go my way *What is the gift here?*

18

full circle

What society does to its children,
so will its children do to society.

— CICERO

You'll bring peace to your past as well as your present and future when you experience the healing that comes when you parent with soul.

June 8, 2002, started out much like any other summertime Saturday. Our family headed to the mall in the neighboring town of Glenwood Springs where we bought a few things before heading to the hot springs pool for an afternoon dip. The winds were strong that day. I remember laughing with my children as we watched someone's float toy rise to the top of a nearby cottonwood tree in a swirling gust.

We saw the first smoke clouds from the pool just after noon. About four o'clock, we headed to the health food store. In the store, the anxiety was palpable. Some tourists talked excitedly about where they could go to catch a better view of the fire. The locals exchanged worried glances. We knew what they didn't know, that Colorado was suffering from its worst drought in years. The parched landscape, the high winds, the dry forecast: a recipe for disaster. We headed home.

What little my girls knew about Colorado fires had them terrified. Eight years before, fourteen firefighters lost their lives fighting a blaze in Glenwood Springs. That tragedy lives on for my children in the form of a local memorial and song that their choir group wrote as a tribute to those firefighters. Their choir was even featured performing the song on a Denver news station and they sing the song every summer at music camp.

The next reports we heard came in around 8 P.M. Local radio stations reported that the recreation center, where we learned how to rock climb, and the mall, where we had been just a few hours before, had burned to the ground. My eight-year-old started sobbing, "I'm scared, I'm scared."

As I held her in my arms, I suddenly flashed back to 1969, when I was seven years old and Hurricane Camille, the biggest storm in the country's history, was approaching Gulfport, Mississippi, where I lived. The TV commentator was shouting, "Get out! Get in your car! Leave! This is really bad!" And then the screen went blank.

My parents told me everything would be all right, but I could feel their terror. We went to my grandmother's house, which was made of brick, and my parents told me to go to bed. "I'm scared!" I cried. "You're fine. Go to bed!" After that exchange, I felt not only terrified, but alone.

We stayed at my grandmother's for a week. My parents owned a rental house by the beach, which Camille had picked up and deposited five blocks away. When we were allowed back into our own house, we had no electricity for two weeks. TV coverage of the clean up brought back the terror, and footage of looters added to my jitters.

One night I got up to go to the bathroom, feeling my way down the dark hall. Suddenly a flashlight shone in my eyes. It was my dad, holding the gun that he kept near his bedside as protection from looters. I peed in my pants.

As I held Alexa 33 years later, I realized I could do for her what my parents weren't able to do for me. I breathed and felt my own fear, old and new, and was able at the same time to feel peaceful and strong for her. I acknowledged her fear and told her truthfully that I thought everything would be all right. She chose to sleep with us for the next several nights.

That weekend, between bulletins about the wildfire, I felt drawn to go back and search the Internet and read accounts about Hurricane Camille. I even found the announcement all the stations were making, and that brought many of the details and emotions back. Clearly, anything I was doing for Alexa I was doing for myself.

THE WAY WE WERE

Take a moment now and think back to your family of origin. If you can, grab a pen and paper and fill in your answers to the following questions as you read them. Don't edit too much of this, just write down the first thing that comes to mind. Beneath each question are some of the typical answers that come up in my parenting workshops. Don't feel as if you need to choose one of those. This isn't a multiple-choice test, but you might be as struck as I was at the range of answers.

Take yourself back to the home you grew up in. As you look around your childhood home, answer the following questions:

Marriage is _____.
- **A commitment essential to family**
- **A burden—to be avoided at all costs**
- **A loving communion**

Families are _____.
- **Happy on the outside, miserable on the inside**
- **Disconnected**
- **A safe haven**

Husbands are _____.
- **Gone**
- **Emotionally and physically overpowering**
- **Providers**

Wives are _____.

- Weak
- Servants
- Supportive and loving caregivers

Children are _____.

- To be seen and not heard
- Not important
- A blessing
- Our guides

I am _____.

- Not in control
- Not understood
- Loved

As you answer these questions for yourself, can you see how you have recreated some of your family-of-origin paradigm in your current family? It's helpful to see how strong these original influences are in our lives today. I know that I have changed many of my unhealthy paradigms about how life works but not without a considerable amount of effort.

Can you appreciate the power of the decisions you made in your childhood and how they affect your life today? These decisions or beliefs are closely held and either remain with us throughout our lives or change with a major effort on our part. This is why it is so important for us, as parents, to help our children form healthy beliefs about families, and in particular, the couple relationship.

CREATING YOUR DREAM

Now, let's focus on the future. Shake off any negativity you may have experienced in the exercise above and take a moment to visualize your dream family. If you could have it any way you wanted, how would *you* fill in the blanks? What is your grandest vision of family life? Go back and answer these questions again.

Don't limit yourself by what is or by what seems possible. Stretch yourself to new limits and fill in your answers.

When you've finished this second exercise, read over your answers and sit for a moment, imagining the life you have just described. Breathe it in. Picture it. Feel it. Hold it with the kind of feeling Neville describes in *Immortal Man:*

> First, have a dream, and by a dream I mean a daydream, a glorious, wonderful daydream. Then ask yourself, 'What would it be like if it were true that I am now the man I am dreaming I would like to be. What would it be like?' Then catch the mood of the wish fulfilled and drench yourself with that feeling. Then for all your tomorrows try to the best of your ability to walk faithful to that assumption, and I am telling you from my own experience, in a way that no one knows, it will come and it will come suddenly.

BRINGING THE DREAM INTO PHYSICAL FORM

Gay Hendricks tells us that vision involves the ability to be comfortable in an imagined future. It's also about being uncomfortable in the *zone of not knowing* that exists between where you are now and where you want to be. Now that you have visualized *your* grandest vision of family life, it's time to focus on the next logical step. Sometimes we set ourselves up for failure by operating at extremes of the continuum. At one extreme, we make a wish, stand back, and hope it will happen. We take little or no action or we take action in erratic spurts. We're too passive. Or at the other extreme, when we commit to so many action steps, it's impossible to succeed at any of them if we're feeling overwhelmed. I suggest a more centered approach: taking the next logical step.

For example, if part of your grandest vision involves making more time for your partner, your next logical step might be scheduling 15 minutes when you can brainstorm how to set aside some couple's time each week. The passive approach might look like it did for me: complaining. First I complained to my husband, then when that did not work, I complained to my friends. Only when I took responsibility for taking the very small but significant step of making time to brainstorm with my husband did we come up with a workable plan for connecting with each other once a week. And, I think, because it started with just the next logical step, our weekly date still remains a part of our practice years later.

So, look at just one area of your grandest vision for your family and backtrack through the logical steps you think it will take you to get from A to Z and commit only to taking step B for now.

If your vision involves more time for yourself, take the next logical step. If it doesn't seem quite right to you, even now, even after all the suggestions in Chapter One to take time for yourself, feel the guilt and do it anyway. "Follow your bliss," as Joseph Campbell says. Part of my dream has been to write this book, and I've taken the next logical steps in tiny increments during the last ten years. I had a folder crammed with notes and clippings for every chapter when I finally sat down to write. Do one thing each day, even if it's small, to move you closer to your dream.

FROM PARENTING CHALLENGE TO PARENTING GIFT

As we move toward our dream, healing ourselves, here's a guideline:

Questions to Transform a Parenting Challenge Into a Parenting Gift

- **Am I feeling connected to myself?**

- **When I think of my vision of my child at 19, how will I wish I had handled this?**

- **Am I remembering to breathe?**

- At what level of the change process am I, in terms of this particular issue?

- Which of my child's *PHIL* needs aren't being met?

- How can I move toward my child with love?

- Am I making connection with my child top priority?

- Am I committing one of the Seven Deadly Disconnects?

- Have I had enough silence lately?

- What is my intuition telling me?

- What have I done to attract this situation?

- What can I appreciate right now about this situation?

- Am I speaking my whole truth? Acknowledging my genuine feelings? Aligning words, thoughts, and actions?

- Am I thinking abundantly?

- Which obstacles to abundance are up for me?

- Am I considering my spouse or partner's needs?

- Am I embracing what is?

Not all of these questions may apply to a given situation, but you get the idea. Here's how I processed a time when I yelled at my children:

Accept What Is	I lost it and yelled at the kids.
Intuition	I listened to my inner guide, who said, "No, not a good idea."
Integrity	I apologized, saying this is not the kind of person I want to be.

What You Want	I looked for the positive, the lesson.
Accept What Is	I forgave myself and changed the tapes in my head, using an uplifting "second thought."
Abundance	I made a new plan for the future.

Use the principles in this book everyday. Make them part of you. Parenting with Soul means reparenting yourself as you parent your child and experience greater peace. As you raise your child and heal yourself, ask these questions:

- **Would I want someone to do this to me?**

- **Would I treat my best friend this way?**

- **How will my child remember me?**

- **What is my child deciding as I act this way?**

- **Would I do this if one million people or my minister were watching?**

- **What could I do that would bring me joy in this moment?**

- **Looking back at this time when my child is an adult, what would I wish I would have said/done?**

As we learn to Parent with Soul, life will hand us new challenges, and with each one we have the opportunity to heal ourselves and to master these principles more deeply and to heal ourselves, and to bring greater peace into the world. As the bumper sticker says, "It's never too late to have a happy childhood." And in the process, we all heal. Measure your success by the amount of joy in your family, not by what your mother-in-law or a book says. What's the look on your child's face when you walk in? And what's the look on yours? All disconnection stems from one primary disconnection—the disconnection to our souls. When we parent with soul, we reconnect and heal ourselves and create future generations of children who will instinctively do the same.

Prayer/Affirmation

In a desperate moment,
The me I was
prayed to whomever would hear,
and the me I would be
reached back in love
took my hand
and led me to be
the me I would be.

In a desperate moment,
The me I would be
prayed to the me I am,
reaching for me,
knowing I would help.

In a desperate moment,
The me I am smiles toward
the me I will be.

And she smiles back at all of us.

— WINNIE SHOWS,
HAIRBALL AND OTHER POEMS OF TRANSFORMATION

Soulful Reminders

- **What we do for our children we do for ourselves.**

- **We formed our ideas about family, marriage, and children when we were children.**

- **You can create your dream family if you clearly visualize it and take the next logical steps.**

- **Apply the principles in this book to change parenting challenges into parenting gifts.**

- **When we Parent with Soul, we reconnect, heal ourselves, and create future generations of children who will instinctively do the same.**

The Power of One Small Step

Write down one practice you learned or were reminded of in this chapter that you will use this week to come full circle. I started by doing for my children what my parents couldn't do for me.

glossary

BUDDHA: Indian philosopher and founder of Buddhism; formulated and taught doctrine of "four noble truths" and "chain of causation." http://www.buddhanet.net

JESUS: The Jewish religious teacher whose life, death, and resurrection as reported by the Evangelists are the bases of the Christian message of salvation.

ABRAHAM-HICKS: Motivational speaker who delivers a message about attaining what you want through dialogue with a group of spiritual teachers who call themselves Abraham. www.abraham-hicks.com

BAN BREATHNACH, SARAH: Author of *Simple Abundance*. www.simpleabundance.com

CAINER, JONATHAN: British astrologer featured in *The Mirror* and on the BBC. www.cainer.com

CARNEGIE, DALE: International lecturer and author of *How to Win Friends and Influence People*. www.dale-carnegie.com

CHOPRA, DEEPAK: Author of *The Seven Spiritual Laws for Parents* and many other books on health and well-being. www.chopra.com

CHOQUETTE, SONIA: Spiritual teacher about intuition and author of *The Wise Child*. www.soniachoquette.com

CHUANG-TZU: A Taoist pantheist, mystic, and humorist during the Chou Dynasty. www.clas.ufl.edu/users/gthursby/taoism/cz-text1.htm

COVEY, STEPHEN: Author of *The Seven Habits of Highly Effective People* and founder of the Covey Leadership Center. www.franklincovey.com

DREIKURS, RUDOLF: Adlerian psychologist and author of *Children: The Challenge* and other books. www.krapu4.com/psy/teach/dreikurs.htm

DYER, WAYNE: Motivational speaker and author of *Your Erroneous Zones* and other books. www.drwaynedyer.com

ECKHART, MEISTER: Sixteenth-century German Dominican mystic.

FOX, EMMET: A popular 1930s metaphysician who was born in Ireland, educated in England, and spent most of his career in the United States. http://website.lineone.net/~cornerstone/emmetfox.htm

GANGAJI: Teacher and author whose message is to end immediately all outward searching and discover directly within your own heart the fathomless truth of who you are. www.gangaji.org

GINOTT, HAIM: Israeli psychologist and parenting expert, author of *Between Parent and Child*.

GOTTMAN, JOHN: Expert on marriage stability and divorce prediction and author of *The Seven Principles for Making Marriage Work*. www.gottman.com

HAY, LOUISE: Metaphysical teacher and author of *You Can Heal Your Life* and other books. www.hayhouse.com

HENDRICKS, GAY: A psychologist who has published over twenty books in the areas of conscious relationship, body/mind integration, and conscious business. www.hendricks.com

HOLMES, ERNEST: Founder of the Church of Religious Science and author of *The Science of Mind*. http://cornerstone.wwwhubs.com/ernestholmes.htm

HUBBARD, ELBERT: Prolific American editor, publisher, and author of the moralistic essay "A Message to Garcia." www.bigeye.com/elberth.htm

JAMES, WILLIAM: Psychologist and philosopher. www.emory.edu/EDUCATION/mfp/james.html

JAMPOLSKY, GERALD G.: Physician and founder of the Center for Attitudinal Healing for people affected by catastrophic illness and author of *Change Your Mind, Change Your Life.* www.localcommunities.org/servlet/lc_ProcServ/dbpage=page&mode=display&gid=0100 4011550947263615155189

KATIE, BYRON: Author of *Loving What Is* and creator of "The Work." www.thework.org

KEATING, THOMAS: Abbot of St. Benedict's Monastery, Snowmass, CO., and author of *Centering Prayer in Daily Life and Ministry.* www.thecentering.org

KVOLS, KATHRYN: Founder of The International Network for Children and Families, teacher and author of *Redirecting Children's Behavior.* www.redirectingbehavior.com

LEWIS, C.S.: Twentieth-century Irish author of *The Chronicles of Narnia.* http://cslewis.drzeus.net

MARCINIAK, BARBARA: Metaphysician and channel of the Pleiadians. www.pleiadians.com

MORRISEY, MARY MANNIN: Founder of the Living Enrichment Center of Wilsonville, OR. www.lecworld.org

NEMETH, MARIA: Founder of the Academy for Coaching Excellence and author of *The Energy of Money.* www.marianemeth.com

PARAMAHANSA YOGANANDA: Founder of the Self Realization Fellowship and the first great Indian spiritual master to live and teach in the West. www.yogananda-srf.org

PEALE, NORMAN VINCENT: One of the foremost motivational speakers of the twentieth century and author of *The Power of Positive Thinking.* www.guideposts.com

RAM DASS: Inspiring teacher and author of *Be Here Now.* http://ramdasstapes.org/index.htm

RAY, SONDRA: Teacher, trainer, healer, and author of *I Deserve Love.* www.breathaware.com/sondra.html

RICHARDSON, CHERYL: Speaker and author of *Take Time for Your Life.* www.cherylrichardson.com

ROMAN, SANAYA AND DUANE PACKER: Channels of Orin and DaBen and authors of *Creating Money.* www.orindaben.com

RUMI: Sufi poet and mystic who founded the Mawlawi Sufi order, a leading mystical brotherhood of Islam. www.khamush.com/life.html

THE DALAI LAMA: His Holiness the 14th Dalai Lama Tenzin Gyatso, head of state and spiritual leader of the Tibetan people. www.tibet.com/DL

THICH NHAT HANH: A Buddhist monk, poet, peace activist, and the author of *The Miracle of Mindfulness* and many other books. www.parallax.org

TOLLE, ECKHART: Counselor, spiritual teacher, and author of *The Power of Now.* www.eckharttolle.com

WALSCH, NEALE DONALD: A modern day spiritual messenger and author of the *Conversations with God* series. www.conversationswithgod.org

WEIL, ANDREW: Founder and director of the Integrative Medicine at the University of Arizona's Health Sciences Center in Tucson and author of *8 Weeks to Optimum Health and Spontaneous Healing.* www.drweil.com

WEISS, RITA: Professor Emerita, Speech, Language, and Hearing Sciences at the University of Colorado in Boulder.

WILLIAMSON, MARIANNE: Spiritual leader of Unity Renaissance Interfaith Spiritual Fellowship, and author of *A Return to Love: Reflections on the Principles of a Course in Miracles.* www.marianne.com

WILSON, BILL: Founder of Alcoholics Anonymous. www.alcoholics-anonymous.org

resources

Chapter One

20-Minute Retreats: Revive Your Spirit in Just Minutes a Day with Simple Self-Led Practices by Rachel Harris, Ph.D. (Owl Books, 2000)

Callings: Finding and Following the Authentic Life by Gregg Levoy (Three Rivers Press, 1998)

Journey to Center: Lessons in Unifying Body, Mind and Spirit by Thomas F. Crum (Fireside, 1997)

Take Time for Your Life: A Personal Coach's Seven-Step Program for Creating the Life You Want by Cheryl Richardson (Broadway Books, 1999)

The Art of Doing Nothing by Veronique Vienne (Clarkson Potter/Publishers, 1998)

Your Best Year Yet! by Jinny S. Ditzler (Warner Books, 2000)

Chapter Two

A Year to Live: How to Live This Year As if It Were Your Last by Steven Levine (Three Rivers Press, 1998)

First Things First: To Live, To Love, To Learn, To Leave a Legacy by Stephen Covey (Fireside, 1996)

Who Am I?: Personality Types for Self-Discovery by Robert Frager, Editor (J.P. Tarcher, 1994)

Chapter Three

Books

Conscious Breathing by Gay Hendricks, Ph.D. (Bantam Books, 1995)

Tapes

Breathing: The Master Key to Self Healing by Andrew Weil, M.D.
(Sounds True, 1999) www.soundstrue.com

Websites

Daily Breath www.dailybreath.com

Ask Dr. Weil www.drweil.com

The Center for Professional Breathwork and Movement
http://www.hendricks.com/pdf/breathing_center.pdf

Chapter Four

Books

Feel the Fear and Do It Anyway by Susan Jeffers, Ph.D. (Ballantine Books,
1987)

*The Dark Side of the Light Chasers: Reclaiming Your Power, Creativity,
Brilliance, and Dreams* by Debbie Ford (Riverhead Books, 1998)

Chapter Five

Books

*Love and Logic Magic for Early Childhood: Practical Parenting from Birth
to Six Years* by Jim Fay, Adryan Russ (Editor) and Foster W. Cline
(Love & Logic Press, 2002)

The Challenge of Parenthood by Rudolf Dreikurs, M.D. (Duell, Sloan,
and Pearce, 1948)

Websites

Reactive Attachment Disorder: It's Time to Understand
http://members.tripod.com/~radclass/

Reactive Attachment Disorder.org
http://www.geocities.com/reactiveattachmentdisorder/

Reactive detachment Disorder and Post-Adoptive Support Ring
http://www.geocities.com/attachmentring/

The Attachment Disorder Site
http://www.attachmentdisorder.net/

Attachment Disorder Network
http://www.radzebra.org/

Chapter Six

Books

Attachment Parenting: Instinctive Care for Your Baby and Young Child by Katie Allison Granju with Betsy Kennedy, R.N., M.S.N. (Pocket Books, 1999)

How To Talk So Kids Will Listen and Listen So Kids Will Talk by Adele Faber and Elaine Mazlish (Avon Books, 1980)

Redirecting Children's Behavior by Kathryn J. Kvols (Parenting Press, 1998)

The Continuum Concept by Jean Liedloff (Perseus Books, 1977)

Unplug the Christmas Machine: A Complete Guide to Putting Love and Joy Back into the Season by Jo Robinson and Jean Coppock Staeheli (Quill, 1991)

Websites

www.redirectingbehavior.com

Family Home Evening Lessons, Activities and Recipes
http://lds.about.com/cs/familynight/

Chapter Eight

Books

Kids, Parents, and Power Struggles: Winning for a Lifetime by Mary Sheedy Kurcinka

Parenting Teens with Love and Logic: Preparing Teens for Responsible Adulthood by Jim Fay and Foster W. Cline (Navpress, 1993)

Positive Discipline by Jane Nelsen (Ballantine, 1996)

Positive Discipline A-Z by Jane Nelsen, Lynn Lott and H. Stephen Glenn

Positive Discipline for Teenagers by Jane Nelsen and Lynn Lott (Prima Publishing, 1994)

Punished by Rewards by Alfie Kohn

Quantity Time: Moving Beyond the Quality Time Myth by Steffen Kraehmer

The Time Bind by Arlie Hochschild

Chapter Nine

Books

Everyday Blessings: The Inner Work of Mindful Parenting by Myla and Jon Kabat-Zinn (Hyperion1997)

Peace Is Every Step by Thich Nhat Hanh (Bantam Books, 1992)

Chapter Ten

Books

Practical Intuition by Laura Day (Villard Books, 1996)

The Wise Child by Sonia Choquette, Ph.D. (Three Rivers Press, 1999)

Trust Your Gut! by Richard M. Contino (Amacom, 1996)

Chapter Eleven

Books

Creative Visualization by Shakti Gawain (Bantam New Age Books, 1983)

Chapter Twelve

Books

Simple Abundance: A Daybook of Comfort and Joy by Sara Ban Breathnach (Warner, 1995)

The Holy Man by Susan Trott (Berkeley Pub Group, 1996)

Chapter Thirteen

Books

Conscious Living: Finding Joy in the Real World by Gay Hendricks (Harper, 2001)

Getting in Touch: The Guide to New Body-Centered Therapies by Christine Caldwell, Ph.D. (Editor), Kern Foundation (Quest Books, 1997)

Practicing Radical Honesty by Brad Blanton, Ph.D., (Sparrowhawk Publications, 2000)

Chapter Fourteen

Books

Creating Money: Keys to Abundance by Sanaya Roman and Duane Packer (H J Kramer, 1998)

From Out of the Blue by Stretton Smith (ISBN: 1889301035)

Rich Dad Poor Dad: What the Rich Teach Their Kids About Money— That the Poor and Middle Class Do Not! by Robert T. Kiyosaki and Sharon L. Lechter (Warner Books, 2000)

The Prayer of Jabez: Breaking Through to the Blessed Life by Rev. Bruce H. Wilkinson (Multnomah Publishers Inc., 2000)

Chapter Fifteen

Books

Anyway by Kent M. Keith and Spencer Johnson (Putnam, 2002)

I Deserve Love by Sondra Ray (Celestial Arts, 1983)

The Energy of Money: A Spiritual Guide to Financial and Personal Fulfillment by Dr. Maria Nemeth (Ballantine Wellspring, 2000)

Anyway, The Paradoxical Commandments: Finding Personal Meaning in a Crazy World by Kent M. Keith (Putnam, 2002)

Chapter Sixteen

Books

Conscious Loving by Gay and Kathlyn Hendricks

Getting the Love You Want by Harville Hendrix

If the Buddha Married: Creating Enduring Relationships on a Spiritual Path by Charlotte Sophis (Charlotte Davis Kasl)

Keeping the Love You Find by Harville Hendrix

Chapter Seventeen

Books

Learning to Love Yourself: A Guide to Becoming Centered by Gay Hendricks (Simon & Schuster, 1993)

Loving What Is by Byron Katie (Harmony Books, 2002)

The Miracle of Mindfulness: An Introduction to the Practice of Meditation by Thich Nhat Hanh (Beacon Press, 1999)

The Power of Now by Eckhart Tolle (New World Library, 1999)

Radical Change, Radical Results by Kate Ludeman, Ph.D. and Eddie Erlandson, M.D. (Dearborn, 2003)

Audio Tapes

Mindfulness Meditation by Jon Kabat-Zinn (Nightingale Conant 1-800-525-9000)

Chapter Eighteen

Your higher power

Your children

You

VICKIE FALCONE is the emerging voice of today's parents. As Founder and Director of the Positive Parenting Network, she helps people create harmonious homes and abundant lives. She is the author of the *Parenting with Soul* course and the *Twelve Months of Positive Parenting* audio subscription series, as well as numerous articles. Merging her skills as seeker, mother, and entrepreneur, she has created a unique blend of practical inspiration that leads to lasting change. She lives high in the Rocky Mountains of Colorado with her husband and two children.

We hope this Jodere Group book has benefited you in your quest for personal, intellectual, and spiritual growth.

Jodere Group is passionate about bringing new and exciting books, such as BUDDHA NEVER RAISED KIDS AND JESUS DIDN'T DRIVE CARPOOL, to readers worldwide. Our company was created as a unique publishing and multimedia avenue for individuals whose mission it is to positively impact the lives of others. We recognize the strength of an original thought, a kind word, and a selfless act—and the power of the individuals who possess them. We are committed to providing the support, passion, and creativity necessary for these individuals to achieve their goals and dreams.

Jodere Group is comprised of a dedicated and creative group of people who strive to provide the highest quality of books, audio programs, online services, and live events to people who pursue life-long learning. It is our personal and professional commitment to embrace our authors, speakers, and readers with helpfulness, respect, and enthusiasm.

For more information about our products, authors, or live events, please call **800.569.1002** or visit us on the Web at **www.jodere.com**

JODERE
GROUP